"Rejoice with me, for I have found my sheep which was lost!" Luke 15:6

The Parables *Christ Told*

Warren Henderson

The Parables Christ Told

By Warren Henderson

Cover Design: Ben Bredeweg
Editing/Proofreading: Dan Macy,
David Lindstrom

Published by Warren A. Henderson
1025 Iron Cap Drive
Stevensville, MT 59870

Perfect Bound ISBN: 978-1-939770-72-1
eBook ISBN: 978-1-939770-73-8

ORDERING INFORMATION:
Copies of *The Parables Christ Told* are available through various online retailers worldwide. Our website address is:
warrenahendersonpublishing.com

Table of Contents

Other Books by the Author

A Heart for God – A Devotional Study of 1 and 2 Samuel
Afterlife – What Will It Be Like?
Answer the Call – Finding Life's Purpose
Be Holy and Come Near– A Devotional Study of Leviticus
Behold the Saviour
Be Angry and Sin Not
Bible Numbers and Symbols
Conquest and the Life of Rest – A Devotional Study of Joshua
Door of Hope – A Devotional Study of the Minor Prophets
Exploring the Pauline Epistles
Forsaken, Forgotten, and Forgiven – A Devotional Study of Jeremiah
Glories Seen & Unseen
Hallowed Be Thy Name – Revering Christ in a Casual World
Hiding God – The Ambition of World Religion
In Search of God – A Quest for Truth
Infidelity and Loyalty – A Devotional Study of Ezekiel and Daniel
Israel's Kings – A Devotional Study of Kings and Chronicles
Knowing the All-Knowing
Managing Anger God's Way
May We See Christ? – A New Testament Journey

May We See Christ? – An Old Testament Journey
May We Serve Christ? – A New Testament Journey
May We Serve Christ? – An Old Testament Journey
Mind Frames – Where Life's Battle Is Won or Lost
Out of Egypt – A Devotional Study of Exodus
Overcoming Your Bully
Passing the Torch – Mentoring the Next Generation for Christ
Relativity and Redemption – A Devotional Study of Judges and Ruth
Revive Us Again – A Devotional Study of Ezra, Nehemiah, and Esther
Seeds of Destiny – A Devotional Study of Genesis
Sorrow and Comfort – A Devotional Study of Isaiah
The Beginning of Wisdom – A Devotional Study of Job, Psalms, Proverbs, Ecclesiastes, and Song of Solomon
The Bible: Myth or Divine Truth?
The Evil Nexus – Are You Aiding the Enemy?
The Fruitful Bough – Affirming Biblical Manhood
The Fruitful Vine – Celebrating Biblical Womanhood
The Hope of Glory – A Preview of Things to Come
The Olive Plants – Raising Spiritual Children
Your Home the Birthing Place of Heaven

Henderson Publishing YouTube Channel

Preface

The four New Testament Gospels reveal one of the most mystifying aspects of the Lord's ministry – the telling of parables. From a cursory view these parables may seem to be perplexing, cryptic, and hard to understand. The Lord told parables in response to questions, self-righteous attitudes, pious murmuring, or as a means of engaging an audience to think more deeply about spiritual matters. On some occasions, the subject matter was so vast the Lord strung several parables together in addressing His listeners, but at other times a single allegory sufficed to portray the intended meaning.

The Lord Jesus intentionally spoke in parables to reveal truth, but in a partially-veiled manner. The parables were not just enjoyable stories but served as a test to the hearers. The casual onlooker, the "window shopper," would hear and not comprehend, nor would he or she desire any more understanding – "thanks for the good story." But those longing to appreciate the spiritual significance of the parable would seek the Lord for further instruction.

It is important to realize that Christ's parables were not intended to develop foundational doctrines of our faith, but to confront smug religiosity and carnal attitudes, and to motivate for righteous living. Much false doctrine has been derived from wrongly interpreting stories that were designed to be ambiguous. The New Testament Epistles expound Church doctrine specifically. Generally speaking, it is observed that the Epistles do not use allegory or metaphorical format to express doctrine. Yet, through the light of the New Testament Epistles the meanings of Christ's parables are more clearly understood and appreciated.

An Overview

When studied individually, the parables that Christ told seem to address a wide range of subjects. Yet, stepping back from the intrinsic meaning of each parable to a panoramic view of the Lord's ministry reveals some interesting patterns in His storytelling. For example, it can be surmised from the collective Gospel accounts that the Lord told no parables for approximately a year and a half after His baptism. Further observation reveals that the Lord spoke only fourteen parables by the close of His Galilean Ministry and eight of these were spoken on one day by the seashore of Galilee. The Lord's Galilean Ministry lasted about two years.

It was not uncommon for several months to pass without any parables being communicated or for several to be spoken all at once. Again, viewing the Gospel accounts collectively, all the parables seem to be spoken on only fifteen different occasions. Interestingly, fifteen of the thirty-nine parables spoken by Christ were conveyed on two occasions. It is also observed that nearly two-thirds of His parables were disclosed in the last seven to eight months of His earthly ministry.

What Is a Parable?

What is a parable? The word "parable" literally means to "cast alongside." Arthur Pink affords a concise definition of a parable:

> The popular definition of Christ's parables is that they were earthly stories with a heavenly meaning. How man gets things upside down! The truth is that His parables were heavenly stories with an earthly meaning, having to do with His earthly people, in earthly connections.[1]

The Lord used a story format to align (cast alongside) a spiritual truth with a common everyday activity the people could relate to, such as sowing seed, using a dragnet for fishing or watching birds feed in a mustard tree. Perhaps the simplest definition of a "parable" is "a heavenly story with an earthly meaning."

Why Did the Lord Speak in Parables?

As mentioned in the Preface, the Lord Jesus intentionally spoke in parables to reveal truth, but in a partially-veiled manner. The parables were not just enjoyable stories but served as a test to the hearers. The casual onlooker, the "window shopper," would hear and not understand, nor would he or she desire any more insight concerning the parable – "thanks for the good story." But those longing to understand the spiritual significance of the parable would seek the Lord for further instruction (e.g., Mark 4:10-12); those who merely enjoyed the story would go their own way. Often it was only the Lord's disciples who sought to learn the deeper meaning of His stories. By design, then, a parable is concealed truth that tests the heart of each one who hears the story.

As the Lord approached the cross, the parable veil thinned, and the meanings became more obvious, even to the dissident. While speaking parables in Jerusalem on the Tuesday before His death, even the Pharisees understood that He was speaking of them.

Christ's Parables in the Gospels

Matthew labors in his account to validate Jesus Christ as the Jewish Messiah. Mark focuses on the busy life of Christ in doing miracles and ministering to the brokenhearted and the down and outers. Mark depicts Christ ministering to God's chosen people, while Matthew reveals Christ as testing Israel. Matthew upholds the kingly assertion in his Gospel, while Luke is careful not to distract from the humanity of Christ and the social appeal of the Savior. Mark contains only four parables, whereas Matthew and Luke contain many more.

It is observed that Matthew meticulously demonstrates that Christ is the culmination of Old Testament prophecies. In contrast, John affirms the deity of Christ in his account and, therefore, repeatedly connects Christ to the completion of Old Testament "types." Interestingly, the word "parable" is found thirty-two times in the four Gospels, but only once in John.

The Greek word rendered "parable" in John 10:6 is *paroimia*, literally meaning "a proverb" or a "figure of speech." J. H. Thayer defines it this way: "a saying out of the usual course or deviating from the usual manner of speaking ... any dark saying which shadows forth some didactic truth, especially a symbolic or figurative saying."[2] The normal Greek word used thirty-one times in the synoptic Gospels is *parabole*, meaning "a similitude implied by a fictitious narrative."[3] The Lord articulated the importance of Himself as the Good Shepherd in John 10; this was not an application-enriched story to prompt the listener to action. Hence, technically speaking, there are no parables found within the Gospel of John.

How Should Parables Be Interpreted?

It is important to realize that the parables were not intended to develop foundational doctrines of our faith, but to address wrong attitudes and to motivate proper living. The New Testament Epistles suffice to expound Church doctrine and generally do not use allegory or metaphorical format to do so, as this format is vague in comparison and can lead to various interpretations. The truth is contained in the whole of Scripture and what is specific and consistent should never be replaced by that which by design is obscure.

The following are suggested rules for properly interpreting a parable:

a. The principal parts and figures of a parable represent certain realities. We should be careful to draw conclusions from these rather than minute details which normally garnish the story, but do not enhance or advance its overall message.

b. Consider only those portions of the parable as allegory that the Lord delineates as so – not the explanation, if given.

c. Interpret a parable that is not explained by looking at similar ones that are. For example, Christ explained that the birds in the first of the seven Kingdom Parables of Matthew 13 represented Satan's opposition to the spread of the gospel message. The meaning of the birds resting in the branches of the mustard tree of the third parable is not explained. However, given what the birds symbolize in the first parable, we can surmise that the birds also represent a negative satanic influence in the Kingdom of Heaven.

d. Interpret the parable in light of its expressed purpose. For example, a lawyer was asking self-justifying questions about salvation, which caused the Lord to respond with a parable (Luke 10:25-37). Accordingly, the main message of the parable should be in keeping with the question that triggered its telling. In this case, the parable caused the lawyer to be made aware of his soul's need and that it could only be satisfied through an unexpected source (Jesus Christ). We must be careful not to interpret specific details of the story beyond its natural meaning. For example, the blood in the story does not represent Christ's blood and the oil mentioned does not represent the Holy Spirit.

What Kinds of Parables Did Christ Tell?

The parables that Christ told can be grouped into four main categories of focus:

- The Mysteries of the Kingdom
- Salvation and Evidence of Salvation
- The Lord's Second Coming and Jewish Attitudes
- Reward for the Faithful

In the eight parables (seven in Matthew and one in Mark) pertaining to unlocking the mysteries of the kingdom, the Lord reveals a chronology of events that would characterize the "kingdom of heaven." These series of parables span the time between His first advent (i.e., His seed-sowing mission on earth) until His return to rule the world in peace and righteousness. Satan is busy in the first four parables undermining the kingdom of heaven (the realm of human profession of God's sovereignty). He attacks the validity of the gospel message, and tries to neutralize the influence of believers on the earth, to corrupt Church leadership and order, and to promote false doctrine within the Church.

However, in the last three parables the enemy is absent and God demonstrates His fathomless grace and power by saving sinners despite what Satan does. Christ paid the great price for the hidden treasure (yet unrepentant and unrestored Israel) and for the pearl (the true Church) and for those Gentiles living through the Tribulation Period who did not bow to the Antichrist or receive his mark.

In the second group of parables, the Lord focuses on important aspects of obtaining salvation by not mixing the law with grace and the necessity of repentance. Then, several parables are spoken to reinforce the *practice* of the believer once his or her *position* in Christ has been secured: forgiving one another, giving unselfishly, loving the Lord and others sacrificially, obeying the word faithfully, and aspiring to live for Christ no matter the personal cost.

The remaining parables largely focus on the Lord's return to the earth and were mainly told in the final four months before His crucifixion. Some of these parables focus on religious pride and Jewish rejection of the Lord and the consequences of that rejection. Others emphasize the rewards for the faithful when the Lord comes into His Kingdom.

For example, in *The Wicked Servant* parable, the Lord punctuates the importance of believers having a future focus and investing into eternity, rather than living for the moment in a world destined to be destroyed. He then informs believers that He will reward them fairly according to how faithful they were to their *opportunities* to serve (the parable of *The Laborers*), their *abilities* given to serve (the parable of *The Talents*) and their *availability* to serve (the parable of *The Pounds*). It is fitting for the Lord to close His parable ministry by speaking of His glorious return to the earth and His faithfulness to reward faithful servants.

This is a summary of the parables that Christ told.

The Mysteries of the Kingdom

Parable Title	Reference
The Sower and the Soils	Matt. 13:5-8; Mark 4:3-8; Luke 8:5-8
The Tares	Matt. 13:24-30
The Mustard Seed	Matt. 13:31-32; Mark 4:30-32; Lk. 13:18-19
The Leaven and the Woman	Matt. 13:33; Luke 13:20-21
The Hidden Treasure	Matt. 13:44
The Pearl of Great Price	Matt. 13:45-46
The Dragnet	Matt. 13:47-50
Mysterious Growth	Mark 4:26-29

Salvation and Evidence of Salvation

Parable Title	Reference
The New Cloth/New Wineskin	Matt. 9:16-17
The Two Houses	Matt. 7:24-27; Luke 6:47-49

The Two Debtors	Luke 7:41-43
The Unforgiving Servant	Matt. 18:23-25
The Good Samaritan	Luke 10:25-37
Friend at Midnight/Fatherhood	Luke 11:5-8
The Rich Fool	Luke 12:16-21
The Great Supper	Luke 14:15-24
The Unfinished Tower/King's Rash War/Salt	Luke 14:28-33
The Lost Sheep	Matt. 18:12-14; Luke 15:4-7
The Lost Coin	Luke 15:8-10
The Lost Son	Luke 15:11-32

The Second Coming and Jewish Attitudes

Parable Title	Reference
The Rude Children	Luke 7:31-35
The Barren Fig Tree	Luke 13:6-9
The Unjust Judge	Luke 18:1-8
The Pharisee & the Tax Collector	Luke 18:9-14
The Two Sons	Matt. 21:28-32
The Landowner & Vinedressers	Matt. 21:33-46; Mark 12:1-12; Lk. 20:9-19
The Marriage Feast	Matt. 22:1-14
The Ten Virgins	Matt. 25:1-13
The Doorkeeper	Mark 13:34-37

Reward for the Faithful

Parable Title	Reference
The Shrewd Manager	Luke 16:1-9
The Servants' Reward	Luke 17:7-10
The Workers in the Vineyard	Matt. 20:1-16
The Minas (Pounds)	Luke 19:11-27
The Two Servants	Matt. 24:45-51; Luke 12:42-48
The Talents	Matt. 25:14-30

Christ's Regional Ministries

It seems likely that Christ's baptism and the subsequent forty days of testing by the devil occurred in late Summer or early Fall of 26 A.D. (this assumes the traditional date of 30 A.D. for Christ's crucifixion). John the baptizer, Christ's forerunner, had already been calling Israel to repentance for some time (perhaps one to two years) when Christ was water baptized and then anointed by the Holy Spirit. After the first cleansing of the temple at Passover (John 2:13-22), Christ departed

Jerusalem through Samaria and returned to Galilee (John 4). At this juncture (the Spring of 27 A.D.), an approximate two-year ministry began throughout Galilee. Capernaum was the Lord's home base of operation during this time.

In the Spring of 29 A.D., the Lord transitioned His ministry to the region of Decapolis, east of the Sea of Galilee. This was a time of specialized ministry for His disciples, some of which were permitted to witness His transfiguration and also see Moses and Elijah attending to Him.

The ministry in Decapolis concluded with the Lord's return to Jerusalem for the Feast of Tabernacles in the Fall of 29 A.D. (John 7:1-8:11). For the next three months, the Lord and His disciples traveled throughout Judea spreading the Kingdom gospel message (Luke 10:1-17). This ministry concluded with the Feast of Dedication (called *Hanukkah* today) in December of that year (John 10:22-39).

The Lord and His disciples spent the next four months mainly in Perea, where John had previously baptized those repenting of their sins (John 10:40-42). It is during the Judean and Perean ministries that the Lord's parable-telling kicked into overdrive. Most of the parables He told occurred during these final months of His earthly sojourn.

Christ and His disciples departed Perea and traveled to Bethany, near Jerusalem, just prior to the Passover feast in 30 A.D. It is at this time that the Lord raises His friend Lazarus from the dead (John 11). This miracle is followed by His triumphant entry into Jerusalem on the colt of a donkey on what is commonly referred to as *Palm Sunday* (John 12:1-19).

The final week of the Lord's ministry on earth was spent confronting stubborn Jewish attitudes and promising reward to those found faithful when He returned to establish His kingdom. The culmination of Christ's earthly ministry then occurred in Jerusalem: His suffering and death at Calvary, and His resurrection from a garden tomb three days later.

The number "2" transposed on the following map of Israel nicely summarizes the movements of our Lord and His disciples while they sought the lost sheep of Israel in a three-plus-year gospel campaign. The base of the "2" is bi-directional, as the Lord returned from Perea (or Peraea) to Jerusalem the final week of His earthly sojourn.

Map of Christ's Regional Ministries: Galilee, Decapolis, Judea, Perea, and Jerusalem

The Mysteries of the Kingdom

Parable Title	Reference
The Sower and the Soils	Matt. 13:5-8; Mark 4:3-8; Luke 8:5-8
The Tares	Matt. 13:24-30
The Mustard Seed	Matt. 13:31-32; Mark 4:30-32; Lk. 13:18-19
The Leaven and the Woman	Matt. 13:33; Luke 13:20-21
The Hidden Treasure	Matt. 13:44
The Pearl of Great Price	Matt. 13:45-46
The Dragnet	Matt. 13:47-50
Mysterious Growth	Mark 4:26-29

The Kingdom of Heaven

The phrase "kingdom of heaven" is found thirty-two times in Matthew but nowhere else in all of Scripture. This peculiarity must be associated with the authority theme of his Gospel (i.e., Jesus Christ is the Messiah and the legitimate heir to the throne of David). The similar and associated term "kingdom of God" is applied fifty-four times in the Gospel accounts, but only appears five times in Matthew and merely twice in John. What is the significance of these phrases, and how do the two terms relate to each other?

Centuries of debate on this subject prove insufficient to answer this question fully. The terms are used interchangeably by the Lord during the Sermon on the Mount and the Lord's discussion with His disciples concerning the rich young ruler who valued his wealth above following the Lord (Matt. 19:23-24). These instances seem to indicate that there is minimal difference in the meaning of the terms, or perhaps, an interrelated meaning where the "kingdom of God" is a subset of the "kingdom of heaven" – the former, representing those who willingly acknowledge and submit to God's sovereignty, and the latter, all those under His rule, whether they acknowledge it or not.

Given this understanding, the "kingdom of heaven" refers to the realm of human profession in which one is given an opportunity to acknowledge God's sovereign rule or "the kingdom of God." C. I. Scofield writes:

> The kingdom of heaven is similar in many respects to the kingdom of God and is often used synonymously with it, though emphasizing certain features of divine government. When contrasted with the universal kingdom of God, the kingdom of heaven includes only men on earth, excluding angels and other creatures. The kingdom of heaven is the earthly sphere of profession as shown by the inclusion of these designated as wheat and tares, the latter of which are cast out of the kingdom (Matt. 13:41), and is compared to a net containing both the good and bad fish which are later separated (Matt. 13:47).[4]

Other commentators, such as William MacDonald, also acknowledge a realm of human profession within the kingdom of heaven, which is composed of true believers and mere professors, but sees no tangible disagreement between the terms "kingdom of heaven" and "kingdom of God." He writes:

> The kingdom of heaven is the sphere in which God's rule is acknowledged. The word "heaven" is used figuratively to denote God; this is clearly shown in Daniel 4:25-26. In verse 25, Daniel said that the Most High rules in the kingdom of men. In the very next verse, he says that Heaven rules. Thus, the kingdom of heaven announces the rule of God, which exists wherever people submit to that rule.[5]

It is important to understand that "kingdom of heaven" and the church are not synonymous terms, for the kingdom of heaven contains both the children of God and the children of the devil, while the universal Church is only composed of true believers. Those who have believed the gospel message experience rebirth and become children of God (John 1:12-13; Eph. 2:1-6).

So, why is the term "kingdom of heaven" unique to Matthew? The Jews would have been familiar with the prophet Daniel's association of "heaven" and "kingdom" terminology in declaring the scene in which the Son of Man (Christ) would return to earth from heaven to establish an everlasting dominion:

> *I was watching in the night visions, and behold, One like* ***the Son of Man****, coming with the clouds of heaven! He came to the Ancient of Days, and they brought Him near before Him. Then to Him was given dominion and glory and* ***a kingdom****, that all peoples, nations, and languages should serve Him.* ***His dominion*** *is an everlasting*

> *dominion, which shall not pass away, and **His kingdom** the one which shall not be destroyed (Dan. 7:13-14).*

Matthew's presentation of Jesus as the Jewish Messiah and Daniel's foretelling of Messiah coming from heaven to establish rightful authority over the Jews combine nicely to speak of the "kingdom of heaven" message (or offer, if you will). Would the Jews acknowledge His claim of authority over them? The term "kingdom of heaven" seems to relate to the presentation of Christ and the decision of the people to accept or reject Him as king. L. Laurenson summarizes the matter:

> The expression "Kingdom of Heaven" is found only in Matthew, and only in Matthew do we get the "Gospel of the Kingdom," and that thrice repeated (Chapters 4, 9, 24). Here was the cure for all the ills that afflicted Jehovah's land, but, alas! Israel refused the Gospel of the Kingdom then, as sinners today refuse the Gospel of Grace. And there never was grace like the grace of Christ.[6]

In the realm of human profession of God's sovereign rule, some reject God's authority over them, others extend mere "lip service" to God, but only those who sincerely believe and submit to God's Word will inherit Christ's kingdom. While the kingdom of heaven contains non-believers and wicked aspects, the true kingdom of God will have none of these things in it. Accordingly, the two terms can be used interchangeably, as long as this distinction is understood.

The Stages of God's Kingdom

There are five main stages of God's kingdom identified in Scripture. The Lord Jesus addressed three of these intervals during a parable series spoken from a boat to a large crowd gathered at the Sea of Galilee (Matt. 13:1-2). The Lord refers to the second kingdom interval in the first parable of *The Sower and the Soils* and the fourth kingdom interval in the last parable of *The Dragnet*; the third kingdom interval is referred to in the remaining parables. The five intervals of God's Kingdom are as follows:

The First Interval: The Kingdom Predicted (Dan. 2:44-45). Daniel's dream predicted that the Stone (i.e., a stone not cut with human hands, representing God's Son) would return to the earth to put down all Gentile rule and establish His kingdom that will last forever.

The Second Interval: The Kingdom at Hand (Matt. 4:17, 12:28). Both John the Baptist and the Lord Jesus announced that the kingdom had arrived. It was offered to the Jews, who largely rejected the King who offered it.

The Third Interval: The Kingdom in Interim (Acts 8:12, 19:18, 20:25). Although the King is absent, His Spirit-filled subjects are living out the kingdom's characteristics (during the Church Age) until the King literally returns to set up His kingdom on earth. The Church Age ends with *The Day of Christ*, which refers to the rapture of the Church and the subsequent evaluation of each believer's works at the *Judgment Seat of Christ*.

The Fourth Interval: The Kingdom Manifested (Rev. 19:11-20:3). During this interval, Christ will return to the earth, defeat the opposing forces, judge the Antichrist, false prophet, and those who took the mark of the beast, put Satan in the bottomless pit, and then reign over the world for a thousand years. The Jewish nation will be forever restored to God at this time. As applied in the New Testament, this interval relates to *The Day of the Lord.*

The Fifth Interval: The Eternal Kingdom (2 Pet. 1:11; 1 Cor. 15:28). Also referred to as *The Day of God* by Peter. The Son will return all things that were degraded by sin back to the Father in perfection. There will be a new heaven and a new earth which will form the *eternal state*.

Christ's kingdom was foretold in the Old Testament, announced first by John the Baptist and then Jesus Christ, but was ultimately rejected by the Jews (i.e., its spiritual aspects and its King). *The Kingdom Parables* of Matthew 13 bridge the gap between the first advent of the Lord to the earth to suffer for our sin and His second advent in which His kingdom will be established and all that is wicked will be removed.

After the Jews rejected Christ's offer of a literal, earthly, political kingdom with Him as King, the kingdom, in its spiritual sense, was then offered to the Gentiles. Consequently, today, God's kingdom rule is evident in the hearts of believers in the Church. This spiritual interim of God's kingdom will conclude at the end of the Church Age, and then the same kingdom offered to the Jews long ago will be physically established on earth at Christ's Second Advent. God's kingdom in its final phase will be the establishment of a new heaven and a new earth; this will be the eternal state of righteousness – *"that God may be all and all"* (1 Cor. 15:28).

Satan is busy in the first four *Kingdom Parables* doing his best to undermine the kingdom of heaven. However, in the latter parables, God demonstrates His fathomless grace, wisdom, and power in saving Israel, the Church, and Tribulation believers despite all that the enemy has done to oppose His plan of salvation. God will establish His kingdom, with Christ as King, despite all that the enemy does to oppose Him.

The Sower and the Soils

> *Then He spoke many things to them in parables, saying: "Behold, a sower went out to sow. And as he sowed, some seed fell by the wayside; and the birds came and devoured them. Some fell on stony places, where they did not have much earth; and they immediately sprang up because they had no depth of earth. But when the sun was up they were scorched, and because they had no root they withered away. And some fell among thorns, and the thorns sprang up and choked them. But others fell on good ground and yielded a crop: some a hundredfold, some sixty, some thirty. He who has ears to hear, let him hear!"* (Matt. 13:3-9).

> *"Therefore hear the parable of the sower: When anyone hears the word of the kingdom, and does not understand it, then the wicked one comes and snatches away what was sown in his heart. This is he who received seed by the wayside. But he who received the seed on stony places, this is he who hears the word and immediately receives it with joy; yet he has no root in himself, but endures only for a while. For when tribulation or persecution arises because of the word, immediately he stumbles. Now he who received seed among the thorns is he who hears the word, and the cares of this world and the*

deceitfulness of riches choke the word, and he becomes unfruitful. But he who received seed on the good ground is he who hears the word and understands it, who indeed bears fruit and produces: some a hundredfold, some sixty, some thirty" (Matt. 13:18-23).

The Jews were a nation composed of shepherds and farmers. So, when the prophets Hosea (Hos. 10:12-13) and Jeremiah (Jer. 4:3) had sternly warned them centuries earlier to plow up their fallow ground, they understood the analogy. Fallow ground is soil that was once cultivated, but now lies waste and is completely fruitless. The longer it remains uncultivated, the harder it becomes; such is the nature of the human heart that rejects God's Word. In order for fallow ground to be made profitable again, it must be broken up with a plow; only then can it be planted and made fruitful. The purpose of this Old Testament soil analogy was to call Israel to repentance. The Lord continues that message in the parable of *The Sower and the Soils*.

The ground in which the seed (God's Word) is sown is likened to the various dispositions of the human heart. Four types of "soils" or hearts are identified: the wayside, stony, thorny, and fruitful ground.

The key components of this parable must be properly identified if we are to understand its meaning:

The seed = the Word of God (specifically the Kingdom message).

The sower = Christ primarily.

The soils = various human hearts (i.e., as God knows them).

The birds = Satan's opposition to God's Word being shared.

The sun = persecution and suffering.

The thorns = the influence of humanism and worldly affairs.

The plant = the visible evidence of God's Word at work.

The fruit = the visible evidence of true salvation.

The wayside = someone with no time for or interest in God's Word.

The stony ground = someone emotionally effected by God's Word.

The thorny ground = those who allowed worldliness to negate the Word.

This parable represents the proclamation and offering of the kingdom to Israel by a sower, who primarily represents Christ, but may include John the baptizer also (Matt. 3:2, 4:17). The seed in the parable is God's Word, which is "living and powerful" (Heb. 4:12). A seed contains life and God's Word offers life to those who will receive in faith. Specifically, the seed in this parable represents the kingdom message offered by Christ to the Jewish nation; this invitation could not be received without genuine repentance. The various soils represent the spiritual disposition of human hearts that God's message would confront. Only those having a softened and prepared heart received God's message and became fruitful to Him.

The birds depict Satan's adverse efforts to oppose the receipt of God's Word once sown among the populace. Birds are often used in Scripture to metaphorically convey satanic opposition. For example, even after Abram had obeyed God's word and prepared animals and birds for an offering, he still had to drive the unclean birds from devouring his sacrifice until later in the day when God confirmed His covenant with Abram (Gen. 15). Satan was opposing God's covenant with Abram and thus the forthcoming Messiah that would come through it – the One who would bless all families of the earth (Gen. 12:3). Likewise, in this parable, the birds symbolize Satan's evil influence and operations to oppose God's kingdom and the efforts of Messiah to establish His kingdom.

Many have interpreted the visible plant in the parable as a sign of conversion and regeneration, but the Lord clarifies in the explanation that is not the case. What is seen above the ground is a counterfeit life because the plant does not have a root of faith below the ground (i.e., in the heart). Only God sees what is in each of our hearts, that is, what is below the ground in the parable. We can only see the outward manifestation of the heart in visible behavior. The plants in this parable represent the visible evidence that the Word of God has had an impact on a person's heart, but it is not necessarily conversion.

Some people feel conviction and guilt after being confronted with the gospel message and respond by self-reformation, rather than by true repentance and acceptance of Christ. In time, trials (intense sunlight) and the cares of the world (the thorns) reveal the true reality of things – no true conversion (no root below ground). In this parable, the plants associated with the stony and thorny ground do not represent true life, but merely an emotional response to God's Word. Only the ground that produced fruit represents a true conversion – there can be no fruitfulness to God unless His seed has produced a root of faith in the human heart.

The Lord Jesus said that you will know a tree (a true believer) by whether he or she bears good fruit (behavior and deeds which honor God) or not (Matt. 7:17-18): *"Therefore by their fruits you will know them"* (Matt. 7:20). This means that at times we may be conned by well-meaning, moral, and Christ-identifying people, but the Lord is not fooled by the facade of an unregenerate person. In fact, the Lord said there are many who know things about Him, but have not trusted Him for salvation, hence, they have not shown Christ to be their Lord (Matt. 7:21-23). Clearly, it is possible to know a lot about the Lord and do things in His name without ever being born again. The Lord knows who are truly His and who the counterfeits are. Many identifying with Christ, even calling Him Lord, are not actually saved. The true test of knowing and serving the Lord is found in our desire to do God's will – this is true fruit-bearing. Only those who do the will of God are really His people (Mark 3:35).

The following summarizes the four kinds of soils identified in this parable. The wayside: The heart that has no interest in the things of God and blatantly rejects the gospel message. The Word had no visible influence on the hearer. The stony ground: The heart in which the Word of God did not penetrate deep enough to cause the reality of new birth. These people are mere professors in religious camouflage; they had an emotional response to the gospel message instead of brokenness and repentance before God. A little suffering shows them for who they really are. The thorny ground: The heart in which the Word of God causes the individual to feel guilt and to change his or her conduct through self-effort, but because there is no true conversion, the cares of the world quickly choke out the effect of God's Word in this life. The good ground: The heart that is well-prepared and receives the Word of God by faith alone unto salvation. True salvation is evidenced by fruit-bearing.

The Wheat and the Tares

> *Another parable He put forth to them, saying: "The kingdom of heaven is like a man who sowed good seed in his field; but while men slept, his enemy came and sowed tares among the wheat and went his way. But when the grain had sprouted and produced a crop, then the*

tares also appeared. So the servants of the owner came and said to him, 'Sir, did you not sow good seed in your field? How then does it have tares?' He said to them, 'An enemy has done this.' The servants said to him, 'Do you want us then to go and gather them up?' But he said, 'No, lest while you gather up the tares you also uproot the wheat with them. Let both grow together until the harvest, and at the time of harvest I will say to the reapers, "First gather together the tares and bind them in bundles to burn them, but gather the wheat into my barn."'"

Then Jesus sent the multitude away and went into the house. And His disciples came to Him, saying, "Explain to us the parable of the tares of the field." He answered and said to them: "He who sows the good seed is the Son of Man. The field is the world, the good seeds are the sons of the kingdom, but the tares are the sons of the wicked one. The enemy who sowed them is the devil, the harvest is the end of the age, and the reapers are the angels. Therefore, as the tares are gathered and burned in the fire, so it will be at the end of this age. The Son of Man will send out His angels, and they will gather out of His kingdom all things that offend, and those who practice lawlessness, and will cast them into the furnace of fire. There will be wailing and gnashing of teeth. Then the righteous will shine forth as the sun in the kingdom of their Father. He who has ears to hear, let him hear!" (Matt. 13:24-30, 36-43).

In this parable the Lord tells of an enemy sneaking in at night and planting tares alongside the wheat the master of the field had sown previously. The tares, or darnel (*Lolium temulentum*), is a prolific weed that looks much like wheat until harvesttime. When wheat matures, it develops a fruit-laden head of grain that bows down before its Creator as it ripens. The darnel has no such fruit-laden head of grain and thereby maintains an upright and haughty disposition before God.

After the tares were discovered, the master told his servants not to uproot the darnel, as that would also damage the wheat. Rather, the matter would be settled at harvesttime. The wheat (i.e., God's children) would be gathered into God's heavenly barn, while the darnel, the children of the devil, would be gathered up by holy angels and cast into eternal fire.

The key components of this parable are:

The laborers = servants of God.

The wheat = true believers – children of God.

The tares = children of the devil.

The field = the world.

The barn = heaven.

The fire = judgment in hell.

If you are doing anything for the Lord, expect the devil to notice and sow his workers right next to you in order to try to neutralize your testimony for Christ or to negate your ministry for Him. God has you right where He wants you in the world (His field), so expect opposition from the enemy until such time that the Lord takes you home (2 Tim. 3:12).

The Mustard Seed

> *Another parable He put forth to them, saying: "The kingdom of heaven is like a mustard seed, which a man took and sowed in his field, which indeed is the least of all the seeds; but when it is grown it is greater than the herbs and becomes a tree, so that the birds of the air come and nest in its branches"* (Matt. 13:31-32).

In this parable the kingdom of heaven is compared to a mustard seed that quickly grew into an herb and then into a tree that birds could build their nests in. The mustard seed would be the smallest seed familiar to the Lord's audience, and represents the humble beginning of the kingdom, when it was relatively small, pure, and fruitful – becoming a fruitful herb as intended. This demonstrated the power of the Holy Spirit to develop and prosper the kingdom through the preaching of the gospel message. This analogy compares well with the first three centuries of the Church Age. Roman oppression during this time had a purifying effect on the Church and resulted in believers taking the message of salvation in Christ alone throughout the empire.

However, the mustard herb continued to grow at a supernatural rate beyond this healthy and fruitful state into a sizeable tree which became home to many birds. The evil birds that stole the seed (the Word of God) in the first parable find a safe haven in the branches of the tree in this parable. This depicts Satan's evil influences in undermining the message, order, and mission given to the Church originally by Christ.

The birds picture the many erroneous religious systems that are associated with Christ's name, but not founded in biblical truth.

Some have suggested that the birds in the branches speak of the kingdom's prosperity, but that is not how the Lord invokes the bird imagery in this parable series. An enemy is present in the first four parables and is opposing God's kingdom. It is not until the crowd disperses and Christ is speaking privately with His disciples that the enemy of the kingdom disappears and God's ability to establish it is declared.

The tree with its many birds represents the condition of the kingdom of heaven in the later days of the Church Age; this reality may be referred to as Christendom. Christendom has many branches and would obviously include the true Church, but also the cults and various humanized movements that promote what is false and corrupt. In the last days, many will identify with Christ, but deny His deity, His headship (including His order for the Church), and His message of salvation. These religious establishments will deny such scriptural teachings as the Godhead (the Trinity), the eternality of the human soul, and the eternal punishment of the wicked.

Today, much of Christendom embraces false doctrine, and ignores God's expressed requirements for church leaders, roles among genders, and the Great Commission. In summary, Christendom, as pictured in the mustard tree, includes the true Church, but also many religious venues and people who are associated with Christ in name only. Christ has no fellowship with what opposes His authority and rule.

The key components of this parable are:

The mustard seed = the simple but powerful gospel message.

The mustard tree = Christendom.

The birds = Satan's corrupting influence on Christendom.

In Revelation 18:2, unclean birds are confined to a cage before being destroyed. During the Tribulation Period, Satan will work through the Antichrist and demonic deception and power to create an apostate religious system that will be ultimately destroyed. Clearly, in whatever age God's people live, they must avoid religious movements which result in unnatural spiritual unions with the world that defile Christ's headship.

The Leaven

Another parable He spoke to them: "The kingdom of heaven is like leaven, which a woman took and hid in three measures of meal till it was all leavened" (Matt. 13:33).

Three symbols, meal, leaven (yeast), and the woman, are used in this parable to depict the progressive corruption of the kingdom by the enemy through false doctrine. Warren Wiersbe summarizes the enemy's effort in this and the previous parable: "The mustard seed illustrates the false *outward* expansion of the kingdom., while the leaven illustrates the *inward* development of false doctrine and false living."[7]

Meal (ground grain) is used to bake bread, a timeless food staple for humanity. Thus, in Scripture, bread is often likened to the receipt of and internalizing of God's Word. Scripture is God's spiritual food for us and without it there can be no spiritual growth. For example, at the end of his life, Moses admonished his countrymen: *"So He [God] humbled you, allowed you to hunger, and fed you with manna which you did not know nor did your fathers know, that He might make you know that man shall not live by bread alone; but man lives by every word that proceeds from the mouth of the Lord"* (Deut. 8:3). The Lord Jesus also affirmed the necessity of internalizing God's Word in order to live for Him (Matt. 4:4). The apostles also taught that believers must feed on God's Word in order to be nourished and strengthened (1 Cor. 3:1-2; Heb. 5:12-14).

Metaphorically speaking, leaven in Scripture is always used to speak of sin, corruption, or evil doctrine (Matt. 13:33; 1 Cor. 5:8). The Lord Jesus warned His disciples against the influence of humanized traditions that oppose sound doctrine: *"Beware of the leaven of the Pharisees, which is hypocrisy"* (Luke 12:1). He also warned them concerning *"the leaven ... of the Sadducees"* (Matt. 16:6). The Sadducees were materialists who denied the existence of the supernatural, the spiritual nature of man, and the idea of a future resurrection. Lastly, the Lord Jesus warned His disciples not to be influenced by *"the leaven of Herod"* (Mark 8:15). Herod, a Jew, was in cahoots with the Roman Empire, and was, therefore, a friend of the world (Jas. 4:4).

Leaven is used to symbolize corruption in the Old Testament also. During the *Feast of Unleavened Bread* the Jews were not to eat leavened bread, nor were they to look upon it, or even have leaven in any of their houses during the seven-day feast (Ex. 13:7).

Despite the consistent negative connotation of leaven in Scripture, some have applied an unscriptural meaning of leaven in this parable in at least two ways. First, after leaven is introduced into the meal, its influence will spread throughout the lump unhindered. This is supposed to represent the unstoppable spread of the gospel through the world. Second, the meal is said to represent all of humanity and the leaven the spread of the gospel; thus the gospel message will spread around the world until everyone is saved. This would be the thinking of those holding a post-millennial view of the Lord's second coming. The main components in the parables must be understood with how each is consistently used in the whole of Scripture or a wrong interpretation of the story will follow. Though these dynamics are reasonable similes of leaven, leaven is never used in Scripture to denote a positive influence.

What does the woman represent in the parable? In a prophetic vision, Zechariah saw a woman restrained in a basket having a lead lid, which was being carried back to Babylon by two winged women. In this scene, the constrained woman symbolizes the idolatry in Israel that God was removing from His people. He was returning this corrupting influence among His people to where it had originated, Babylon.

In God's original plan, woman was created to be Adam's helper and companion; however, she led Adam to disobey God in Eden (Gen. 3:1-6). Likewise, as seen throughout Israel's history, foreign women often enticed Jewish men to depart from the Lord and to embrace false gods (e.g., Num. 25:6-8). So, although women are no more inherently wicked than men, a woman is used at times in the Bible to picture an evil or seductive influence on men (e.g., Rev. 2:20). This highlights the spiritual weakness of men to be seduced into error by sensual means. For this reason, we observe systems of evil being assigned to expressions such as *"the daughter of Zion"* and *"the daughter of Babylon"* (Zech. 2:7; Jer. 6:2).

The key components of this parable are:

The leaven = the introduction of and spreading sway of corruption.

The meal = God's Word – God's food for His people.

The woman = wickedness or evil influence.

Learning of the opposition to the kingdom in the previous three parables and the symbolic meanings of the meal, leaven, and the woman permits us to properly understand this parable: The enemy is introducing evil into good meal to corrupt the food of God's people. By design, this parable follows the imagery of an advanced state of the kingdom, as pictured in the mustard tree – Christendom. This means that, in the latter days of the Church Age, we should expect a number of unsound Bible translations and theological frameworks to be misleading. Satan will readily attack God's Word (Scripture) by perverting, changing, and diluting it.

The enemy knows that if he can corrupt the food of God's people, they will not thrive spiritually. Thankfully, as shown in Zechariah's vision, God is quite capable of limiting and removing wicked influences and corruption from among His people. The Lord's people need not be deceived, for God has preserved His truth for us in Scripture to live by.

The Hidden Treasure

> *Again, the kingdom of heaven is like treasure hidden in a field, which a man found and hid; and for joy over it he goes and sells all that he has and buys that field* (Matt. 13:44).

The crowd dispersed after the telling of the fourth parable. The remaining parables in Matthew 13 were spoken privately by the Lord to His disciples. There was an enemy present in the previous parables, but he is gone also in the final *Kingdom Parables*. It was as if the Lord was saying to His disciples, there has been much opposition to God's kingdom, but now let me tell you the rest of the story. The final parables symbolize how God will save refined Israel, the Church, and Tribulation saints despite what the enemy does!

The parable of *The Hidden Treasure* addresses God's relationship with His covenant people (Israel) and His plan for saving and restoring a refined Jewish remnant to Himself in a future day. God has and does consider Israel a special treasure to Himself (Ex. 19:5; Ps. 135:4). Moses reminded his countrymen of this fact again before his death and their entrance into Canaan – their inheritance from God:

> *Also today the Lord has proclaimed you to be His special people, just as He promised you, that you should keep all His commandments, and that He will set you high above all nations which He has made, in praise, in name, and in honor, and that you may be a holy people to the Lord your God, just as He has spoken* (Deut. 26:18-19).

The prophet Zechariah proclaimed that any nation which harms the Jewish people (beyond what God permits for discipline) will ultimately be judged by God: *"For thus says the Lord of hosts, 'He sent Me after glory, to the nations which plunder you; for he who touches you touches the apple of His eye'"* (Zech. 2:8). The Jews are the apple of God's eye.

Because of Israel's past stubborn idolatry, God did punish His people and scatter them among the Gentile nations (Ezek. 36:16-26). However, after several centuries of being dispersed, the Lord Jesus came into the world to personally offer the kingdom to the Jewish people, but they rejected His offer. Thus, the treasure (the Jewish nation) was found by Christ, and then hidden again after they rejected His Kingdom message. The Lord then bought the entire field (the world) which contained the hidden treasure for His own. As God's Lamb for sacrifice, Christ paid the price for the sin of the world at Calvary by shedding His own blood (John 1:29; Heb. 2:9; 1 Jn. 2:2). Today, the Jewish people remain scattered throughout the world. But in a coming day, Christ will return to reclaim His treasure, His purchased possession, and the spiritually revived Jewish nation will never be lost in the world again.

The key components of this parable are:

The land or field = the world – where Jewish people reside.

The man that bought the field = Christ.

The payment for the field = Christ's judgment at Calvary.

The hidden treasure = the Jewish nation (Israel).

This parable highlights the rejection of Christ and the resulting spiritual blindness of the nation of Israel (Rom. 11:7; 2 Cor. 3:14-15). Israel was cut off from God for rejecting Christ, who then began to woo a Gentile bride for Himself. Israel, the treasure, was consequently hidden again among the nations of the world. Yet, at the Lord's second coming to the earth, He will be gladly accepted by the Jewish nation (Zech. 12:10), and the Jewish people will then receive the Holy Spirit and be restored to God as His people forever. God will regather the Jews to the land of Israel; He will not leave one of them among the nations (Ezek. 39:28-29). In that day, God's *peculiar treasure* will be fully recovered.

The Pearl of Great Price

> *Again, the kingdom of heaven is like a merchant seeking beautiful pearls, who, when he had found one pearl of great price, went and sold all that he had and bought it* (Matt. 13:45-46).

This parable represents the Kingdom in relationship to the Church. The Church Age is the Kingdom in its interim spiritual state. The Church is not the same as the Kingdom, as the Church will be removed from the earth before Christ returns to establish His kingdom on earth. Then the Church will rule and reign with Christ during the Kingdom Age (Rom. 8:17; 2 Tim. 2:12), as will the Tribulation saints (Rev. 20:4).

In His story, the Lord Jesus said that there was a merchant searching for beautiful pearls to purchase. One day he found one superb pearl that he had to have, no matter the cost. He went and sold everything he had to purchase that one exquisite pearl.

Pearls come from oysters which dwell in the sea. When spoken of metaphorically, seas in Scripture typify the Gentile nations (Rev. 17:1, 15). While gems usually gain value when properly cut, pearls only have value in their entirety. In the Lord's mind, there is one particular special pearl (the Church), coming from the seas (i.e., the Gentile nations), which must be His in its complete wholeness. To secure and preserve this pearl, the Lord gave His all, including His life at Calvary to purchase it (2 Cor. 5:19).

The key components of this parable are:

The merchant = Christ.

The great price = Christ's judgment at Calvary on our behalf.

The pearl = the Church.

This lovely allegory is further enhanced when we understand that pearls are created by the oyster's natural response to an irritation within its shell, such as a grain of sand. The pearl slowly forms around the grain of sand and may require as much as four years to fully develop. The sacrifice of Christ at Calvary is the means by which He is likewise slowly building His Body, the Church, saved souls mainly from Gentile nations, but with a few Jews trusting in Him also.

Christ is at the center of everything that the Church is and does. The Church has value only in its full oneness; from a relationship standpoint, the Lord cannot lose part of His Body and still be complete (Eph. 4:4, 15-16). Perhaps this is why there are twelve gates of pearl in the capital city heaven, the New Jerusalem: Whosoever will from any nation on earth can enjoy eternal communion with God through Christ.

The Dragnet

> *Again, the kingdom of heaven is like a dragnet that was cast into the sea and gathered some of every kind, which, when it was full, they drew to shore; and they sat down and gathered the good into vessels, but threw the bad away. So it will be at the end of the age. The angels will come forth, separate the wicked from among the just, and cast them into the furnace of fire. There will be wailing and gnashing of teeth* (Matt. 47-50).

This parable represents the kingdom in relationship to the Gentiles who are saved during the Tribulation Period. The net represents the influence of the kingdom gospel that will be preached by the faithful during the Tribulation Period (Matt. 24:14). This message consists of a warning not to worship the Antichrist and a declaration that judgment of the wicked and Christ's kingdom are coming soon (Rev. 14:6-12).

The fish caught in the sea represent surviving Gentiles who lived through the Tribulation Period. As previously mentioned, seas figuratively represent Gentile nations in Scripture (Rev. 17:1, 15). The sorting of the good and the bad caught in the dragnet refers to the gathering of survivors by the angels to stand before Christ in *The Judgment of the Nations.* This same judgment is spoken of in Matthew 25:31-46, but in that passage, Christ is actively separating the sheep (Tribulation saints) from the condemned goats (the followers of the Antichrist). The meaning is the same: "the good" in this parable and "the sheep" in Matthew 25 will enter Christ's kingdom of peace, blessings, and righteousness.

This activity is also pictured allegorically in Daniel 2:35, 44-45 and has its literal prophetic fulfillment in Revelation 19:20 at Christ's second coming to the earth. In the latter reference, Christ ensures that "the bad," all those who followed the Antichrist (i.e., those who took his mark) and persecuted the Jews are executed and committed to eternal judgment by an angel escort – these people will not enter Christ's kingdom.

The key components of this parable are:

The sea = the Gentile nations.

The dragnet = being divinely gathered for judgment.

The fishermen ("they") = the holy angels.

The sorting = the Judgment of the Nations by Christ.

The good = the Tribulation saints.

The bad = the followers of the Antichrist.

The furnace of fire = Hell.

In summary, the net represents the outcome of preaching the kingdom gospel worldwide during the Tribulation Period (Matt. 24:14). This message consists of a warning to people not to worship the Antichrist because Christ is coming soon to judge the wicked and establish His kingdom (Rev. 14:6-12). The net's contents represent those Gentiles who survived the Tribulation Period and the holy angels will ensure that no one will escape Christ's judicial authority. *The Judgment of Nations* is done suddenly and the general populace will not be expecting it (Matt. 24:36-41). Those unfit for the kingdom (i.e., those who ignored the Kingdom Gospel message) will be abruptly removed from the earth.

Mysterious Growth

And He said, "The kingdom of God is as if a man should scatter seed on the ground, and should sleep by night and rise by day, and the seed should sprout and grow, he himself does not know how. For the earth yields crops by itself: first the blade, then the head, after that the full grain in the head. But when the grain ripens, immediately he puts in the sickle, because the harvest has come" (Mark 4:26-29).

This parable closely aligns with the first Kingdom Parable in Matthew 13 – *The Sower and the Soils*. The kingdom of heaven contains the realm of profession: some will hear and receive the Kingdom message, while others will reject it. It is noteworthy that the man sowing the seed is also the one who raises the sickle to gather the harvest into the barn.

The key components of this parable are:

The seed = the Word of God (the gospel message).

The sower = Christ primarily (the disciples secondarily).

The ground = lost souls residing in the world.

The seed's mysterious growth = the work of the Holy Spirit.

The harvest = the ingathering of saved souls to heaven.

In the parable of *The Sower and the Soils*, Christ is seen as the primary sower and indeed, He is the one who will return to harvest those who are His from the earth. The Holy Spirit illuminates the minds of those who hear the gospel message so that they may come under conviction for their sin and understand their guilt before God. In this fashion, the Holy Spirit woos condemned sinners to Christ for salvation. Those who repent and respond in faith are regenerated by the Holy Spirit (1 Cor. 6:11; Tit. 3:5) and are waiting to be harvested from the earth by Christ.

While this seems to be the primary meaning of the parable, the Lord may have told this parable to encourage the disciples and future disciples to labor hard for the harvest to come. Perhaps this is why the parable is only recorded in Mark's Gospel, which presents the lowly Servant of Jehovah exhausting Himself to serve others. In this view, the sower of the seed (the one preaching that salvation is in Christ) does not know who will believe the message and be spared judgment or who will reject it and remain in their natural condemnation as a descendant of Adam (John 3:18; Rom. 5:12).

The one testifying of Christ to others does not fully understand the work of the Holy Spirit, the process of spiritual growth, nor what it will be like to be with Christ in heaven, yet he or she faithfully shares what they do know and are willing to leave the outcome with God. We can have confidence that when God's Word is shared with others, it will not return void (Isa. 55:11), for His words are *"spirit, and ... life"* (John 6:26).

Only the Holy Spirit can convict people of their sin, and need of righteousness before God (John 16:7-10). Only He can bring them to saving faith and give them the assurance that they are children of God – that is His business (Rom. 8:16). Believers are accountable to be witnesses for Christ in the world (Acts 1:8) and to share the gospel message as they are going from place to place (Matt. 28:19). We must do what we are supposed to do, so that God will do only what He can – save sinners! When the harvest of souls is full and ripe, Christ will come and gather what is His to Himself in heaven (1 Thess. 4:13-18).

Reflecting on Kingdom Truth

After speaking the seventh Kingdom Parable recorded in Matthew 13, the Lord asked His disciples if they had understood *all* that He had told them. Their reply of "yes" is surprising, as the Lord had supplied them a lot new information and He had only explained the meaning of the first, second, and seventh parables. Certainly, the disciples did not comprehend the full implications of all that the Lord Jesus had just taught them in allegory. Their questions to Him later prove this assessment to be true (e.g., Matt. 16:6-12).

Regardless, in addition to Old Testament Scripture, the disciples had now been entrusted with new revelation from Christ. Their stewardship of divine truth was likened to that of a householder who could show off both old and new treasures stored in his home (Matt. 13:52). The disciples were to dispense in tandem both Old Testament truth and the principles of truth just received, the latter being the fulfillment of the former. The *new* is in the *old* contained, but by the *new* the *old* is explained. Truth cannot contradict itself, but the new revelation given by Christ to His disciples would enable them in time to understand what had been previously prophesied in Scripture.

Salvation and Evidence of Salvation

Parable Title	Reference
The New Cloth/New Wineskin	Matt. 9:16-17
The Two Houses	Matt. 7:24-27; Luke 6:47-49
The Two Debtors	Luke 7:41-43
The Unforgiving Servant	Matt. 18:23-25
The Good Samaritan	Luke 10:25-37
Friend at Midnight/Fatherhood	Luke 11:5-8
The Rich Fool	Luke 12:16-21
The Great Supper	Luke 14:15-24
The Unfinished Tower/King's Rash War/Salt	Luke 14:28-33
The Lost Sheep	Matt. 18:12-14; Luke 15:4-7
The Lost Coin	Luke 15:8-10
The Lost Son	Luke 15:11-32

In this second group of parables, the Lord reveals important aspects of salvation such as not mixing the law with grace and the necessity of repentance to receive salvation. Then several parables reinforce the *practice* of the believer once his or her *position* in Christ is secure (e.g., forgiving, giving, obeying, and loving each other and the Lord).

The New Cloth and New Wineskin

> *As Jesus passed on from there, He saw a man named Matthew sitting at the tax office. And He said to him, "Follow Me." So he arose and followed Him. Now it happened, as Jesus sat at the table in the house, that behold, many tax collectors and sinners came and sat down with Him and His disciples. And when the Pharisees saw it, they said to His disciples, "Why does your Teacher eat with tax collectors and sinners?" When Jesus heard that, He said to them, "Those who are well have no need of a physician, but those who are sick. But go and learn what this means: 'I desire mercy and not sacrifice.' For I did not come to call the righteous, but sinners, to repentance."*

> *Then the disciples of John came to Him, saying, "Why do we and the Pharisees fast often, but Your disciples do not fast?" And Jesus said to them, "Can the friends of the bridegroom mourn as long as the bridegroom is with them? But the days will come when the bridegroom will be taken away from them, and then they will fast. No one puts a piece of unshrunk cloth on an old garment; for the patch pulls away from the garment, and the tear is made worse. Nor do they put new wine into old wineskins, or else the wineskins break, the wine is spilled, and the wineskins are ruined. But they put new wine into new wineskins, and both are preserved"* (Matt. 9-17).

This parable was spoken in the house of Matthew (a newly called disciple) in or near Capernaum. This was likely the first parable that Christ spoke and was shared in response to John's disciples' question about fasting. The Lord affirmed that His disciples were not given to fasting because the bridegroom (Himself) was still with them, but soon He would not be – then they would regularly fast. His answer indicated that a new dispensation was coming.

A dispensation in Scripture is not an era of time per se, but rather an economy of truth that God reveals to man and holds him accountable to obey. Dispensations do have their outworking in time and may overlap to some extent. For example, the dispensation of human government established in Genesis 9 was concurrent with the dispensation of the Law instituted with Israel at Mount Sinai and is still in effect during the present dispensation of grace (i.e., the Church Age).

The Lord cited two examples, a new cloth on an old garment and new wine in old wineskin, to show that the purposes of the dispensations of the Law and of Grace were quite different. The Law of Moses was rigid in that, if broken, it did not offer mercy, only condemnation. Accordingly, Paul explains that the purpose of the Law was to show sin (Rom. 3:20) and point guilty sinners to the solution – Christ (Gal. 3:24). The Law only brought condemnation, as no one could keep all of its precepts. But grace through Christ was offered to those who realized that they had fallen short of God's righteousness and needed to be justified by Him to be acceptable before Him (1 Tim. 2:3-6). Grace is receiving the unmerited favor of God.

In summary, lost souls may approach God through law-keeping (i.e., by self-justification) and be found wanting, or by humbly acknowledging their sinful state and receiving redemption and justification through Christ by grace. Consequently, the purpose of both parables was to show that one can choose to live by the Law or by grace, but not both; the two systems cannot be mixed. The purpose of the first was to show the necessity of the second for salvation.

Both parables illustrate this point. A piece of new cloth (unshrunk material) is a poor patch for an old garment, for after it becomes wet and dries, it will shrink and pull away from the old cloth. The latter situation creates a worse outcome than the original problem. Likewise, those trying to mix efforts of self-reformation with God's work of grace will become more resistant to the truth of the gospel message, which has its basis in grace alone.

For the same reason, putting new wine in old wineskin (which has no elasticity) will result in a bad outcome. As the new wine ferments, it will expand and burst the old wineskin, making it unusable. It would have been better to hold to the law alone than to try to mix Law-keeping with God's grace for salvation. Grace plus a nickel is not grace!

The Law was stringent and rigid; its purpose was to condemn, not to save. The Law was designed to highlight man's lost state before God and show his need for God's Savior. Because Christ was born under the Law and completely kept the Law, He was proven an acceptable substitute for sacrifice on the account of the guilty (i.e., everyone). Through the process of substitution, then, God was able to righteously judge human sin and offer forgiveness and acceptance through Christ. This means that those who resort to Law-keeping to earn God's favor instead of believing in Christ's redemptive work alone are telling God, "Your Son did not do enough to save me; you need my help too." This is an offensive notion to God.

Besides the clear meaning of the parables, there is an application that Christians today do well to heed. It is our tendency to want to surround ourselves with pious ornaments to feel like we have had a religious experience. Christendom often pulls in elements and terminology from the Old Testament economy (the Mosaic Law) to create a religious ambiance during church gatherings. Speaking of the church building as "the house of God," for example, is incorrect. The Christian's sanctuary is in heaven now, not the auditorium of an earthly building. In the Old Testament, the temple was the house of God, but in the New Testament the house of God is a spiritual building called the Church – God dwells in His people, not just with them, as in the Old

Testament (1 Tim. 3:5). This means that all believers are able priests now to worship God at any time (1 Pet. 2:5), whereas the Levitical economy permitted only the sons of Aaron before the Lord at certain times.

Accordingly, the use of special robes, lamps/candles, incense, and altars do not belong in the *Dispensation of Grace*. These former religious relics tend to distort our focus of Christ's centrality in our gatherings. This is why the Lord instituted something new, the Lord's Supper, with the emblems of bread and wine, to remind us of Him and His sacrifice for us. Let us be careful of mixing any elements of the Law with all that God wants us to appreciate in grace!

The Two Houses

> *Therefore whoever hears these sayings of Mine, and does them, I will liken him to a wise man who built his house on the rock: and the rain descended, the floods came, and the winds blew and beat on that house; and it did not fall, for it was founded on the rock. But everyone who hears these sayings of Mine, and does not do them, will be like a foolish man who built his house on the sand: and the rain descended, the floods came, and the winds blew and beat on that house; and it fell. And great was its fall* (Matthew 7:24-27).

This parable concluded the Lord's *Sermon on the Mount* address which occurred early in His Galilean ministry, not long after the *New Cloth and New Wineskin* parable was spoken. The purpose of this parable was to verify that true disciples obey and live by God's Word, rather than following their emotions, secular philosophies or tenets of humanism.

The Lord had just informed His audience that the way leading to destruction was wide and the way leading to life was narrow, which meant few would find it. He also had just taught them that there were true and false teachers and also true and false professors. Hence, the parable of the two houses posed two types of builders, one that chose a good foundation to build a house on and the other a poor foundation.

Christ is the Rock in the parable, and true disciples must base their faith on Christ's teachings and live accordingly. This is the stable bedrock to build one's house, or life, upon. The believer is to judge his or her *feelings* out of his or her personal *faith* which was derived from the *fact* of Scripture. If we allow our experiences and feelings to derive our faith, then what we believe will be used to wrongly interpret the meaning of Scripture. The house (i.e., the life) that is built on the foundation of Scripture can weather life's storms of adversity. However, the house with a foundation on the sand will not survive such testing. The foundation of sand represents a life lived for the present, for self, by sight, and based on feelings and relativism. A true disciple of Christ continues to obey Christ's commandments (John 8:31) and only love for Him will cause us to live for Him (John 14:15).

The Two Debtors

> *And Jesus answered and said to him, "Simon, I have something to say to you." So he said, "Teacher, say it." "There was a certain creditor who had two debtors. One owed five hundred denarii, and the other fifty. And when they had nothing with which to repay, he freely forgave them both. Tell Me, therefore, which of them will love him more?" Simon answered and said, "I suppose the one whom he forgave more."*
>
> *And He said to him, "You have rightly judged." Then He turned to the woman and said to Simon, "Do you see this woman? I entered your house; you gave Me no water for My feet, but she has washed My feet with her tears and wiped them with the hair of her head. You gave Me no kiss, but this woman has not ceased to kiss My feet since the time I came in. You did not anoint My head with oil, but this woman has anointed My feet with fragrant oil. Therefore I say to you, her sins, which are many, are forgiven, for she loved much. But to whom little is forgiven, the same loves little." Then He said to her, "Your sins are forgiven." And those who sat at the table with Him began to say to themselves, "Who is this who even forgives sins?" Then He said to the woman, "Your faith has saved you. Go in peace"* (Luke 7:40-50).

A Pharisee named Simon invited the Lord to his home in Capernaum for a meal and the Lord accepted the invitation. While they were eating, a woman of ill repute came into the house with an alabaster flask of fragrant oil. The weeping woman washed the Lord's feet with her tears and wiped them clean with her hair. She then kissed the Lord's feet and anointed them with fragrant oil. The woman was publicly showing her appreciation for Christ; she believed His message of reconciliation.

Most roads were unpaved at this time and the normal footwear of the day was sandals. This meant that the feet of those traveling on foot often became caked with dust or mud. For this reason, it was customary for the host to provide a servant to wash the feet of those who had arrived at his home or at least some provision for washing up, but Simon had not done so. But the woman saw the opportunity to refresh the Lord and did what Simon had failed to do.

However, because of her sinful background (i.e., prostitution), Simon thought less of the Lord for willfully receiving her expression of gratitude: "Surely, if this man was a really a prophet of God, he would know the depravity of this woman and would shun her, instead of welcoming her actions."

As shown by the woman in the parable, a kiss was a symbol of true repentance – she was honoring God's Son in an appropriate way. In contrast, Judas rejected Christ's Lordship and betrayed the Lord with the sign of a kiss (Matt. 26:49). To refuse God's offer of salvation in His Son results in God's judgment, but Judas committed a greater offense: He mocked God's Son by a sign of affection and repentance in order to have him arrested and abused.

The final three verses of Psalm 2 relate to the Holy Spirit's work to reconcile sinners to God. God had already revealed His Son to the nations earlier in that poem; humanity would be wise to fear and serve Him. The Aramaic word *bar* is rendered "son," a term the Gentiles would understand to mean "the rightful heir." Repentance would be demonstrated by those who choose to *"kiss the Son"* (Ps. 2:11). Ultimately, every individual must decide whether they will respect the One God loves and honors, His Son, or be wise in their own conceit.

Returning to the narrative, the Lord, who overheard Simon's thoughts about Him, told him this story about differing responses of two forgiven debtors to rebuke his cold-hearted attitude. The woman, an outcast of society with few resources, had done much more to refresh Him than influential Simon had done even though he was the host. The Lord called Simon's attention to her good works: *"Do you see this woman?"* He then told the woman that though her sins were many, they had been forgiven. *"Your faith has saved you. Go in peace."*

The woman's testimony was used to rebuke Simon in two ways. First, James tells us that "*Faith by itself, if it does not have works, is dead*" (Jas. 2:17). Simon may have been curious about what Jesus was teaching, but his actions showed that he had not trusted in His message or he would have demonstrated his appreciation for being forgiven also. Second, the Lord affirmed *"to whom little is forgiven, the same loves little"* (Luke 7:47)! The portion that we return of what we have received from the Lord directly reflects how much we believe we have been forgiven and how much we love Christ. In summary, those forgiven much – love and give much!

The Unforgiving Servant

> *Jesus said to him, "I do not say to you, up to seven times, but up to seventy times seven. Therefore the kingdom of heaven is like a certain king who wanted to settle accounts with his servants. And when he had begun to settle accounts, one was brought to him who owed him ten thousand talents. But as he was not able to pay, his master commanded that he be sold, with his wife and children and all that he had, and that payment be made. The servant therefore fell down before him, saying, "Master, have patience with me, and I will pay you all." Then the master of that servant was moved with compassion, released him, and forgave him the debt.*
>
> *But that servant went out and found one of his fellow servants who owed him a hundred denarii; and he laid hands on him and took him by the throat, saying, "Pay me what you owe!" So his fellow servant fell down at his feet and begged him, saying, "Have patience with me, and I will pay you all." And he would not, but went and threw him into prison till he should pay the debt. So when his fellow servants saw what had been done, they were very grieved, and came and told their master all that had been done. Then his master, after he had called him, said to him, "You wicked servant! I forgave you all that debt because you begged me. Should you not also have had compassion on your fellow servant, just as I had pity on you?" And his master was angry, and delivered him to the torturers until he should pay all that was due to him. So My heavenly Father also will do to you if each of you, from his heart, does not forgive his brother his trespasses* (Matt. 18:22-35).

This parable was spoken in Capernaum towards the end of Christ's Galilean Ministry, about a year before Calvary. The story was told in response to Peter's question as to how often they should extend forgiveness to someone requesting it. Peter thought seven times was sufficient to demonstrate grace, but the Lord had a quite different idea. He said that "seventy times seven" was a better disposition to have. The Lord was not suggesting that forgiveness should be limited to 490 infractions, but rather, by combining the two numbers, we are to maintain an open-ended attitude.

Paul gives us the motivation to release the offenses of others immediately when we have been wronged: *"And be kind to one another, tenderhearted, forgiving one another, even as God in Christ forgave you"* (Eph. 4:32). Releasing the offenses of others to God frees our minds to serve God appropriately. Because we fully trust Him to handle the situation, we move these released offenses from the foreground to the background of our minds; this permits us to live for God without being hindered by them. Believers are to have a releasing spirit and are to not limit mercy if the offender admits his or her wrongdoing and asks to be forgiven. At such times we are commanded to declare forgiveness to the offender (Luke 17:3-4). We are to maintain such matters in the background of our minds until we can verbally declare forgiveness to the repentant, then the matter should be forgotten. Given what we have been forgiven by Christ, we are not to withhold forgiveness from others when they have repented of the wrongdoing and asked to be forgiven.

The story reveals the proud heart of the debtor in several ways. First, he was sorry that he got caught embezzling his master's wealth, but he did not acknowledge his sin or ask for forgiveness – he merely asked for mercy (because he did not want to be imprisoned for life).

Second, the debt he owed was enormous. At this time, the region of Galilee's total annual revenue was only about 300 talents, and this man owed over thirty-three times that amount.[8] This total debt would equate to billions of U.S. dollars in today's economy and there was no way that he could ever hope to work and repay it. These two behaviors indicate that the embezzler's motives were fostered in pride and insincerity.

Third, after experiencing the king's immense mercy through forgiveness, he was unwilling to forgive another who owed him merely 100 denarii. This was pocket change in comparison to the debt the man had just been forgiven, yet he grabbed the debtor by the throat and demanded payment in full. The debtor begged for mercy and asked for more time in order to repay his account, just as the forgiven servant had done before the king. But the forgiven servant would not relent – he wanted what was his and he wanted it immediately. Unable to pay, the man owing the smaller debt was put into prison until his account could be settled.

The king's actions reflect God's merciful character in wanting to grant forgiveness to those who are undeserving of it. He is a God of tender mercies who is slow to anger and quick to forgive. The embezzler rightly deserved to be thrown into prison, but when the king heard the guilty party beg for mercy, he was prompted to forgive him, erase the enormous debt, and not put him in prison.

However, the king's servants who understood and appreciated their master's merciful spirit were outraged by the incident and informed the king. God is also just, so when the king heard that the forgiven thief had coldly cast a fellow servant into prison over a minor debt, the servant was called before the king again. The king sharply rebuked his "wicked servant" with a question: *"Should you not also have had compassion on your fellow-servant, just as I had pity on you?"*

The thief had not responded properly to the king's mercy and thus invoked his wrath. The unforgiving man was thrown into prison until he could pay his original debt, which was approximately 600,000 times greater than the debt he was unwilling to forgive. In the end, he did receive immediately what was his – the enormous debt that he had no hope of ever repaying. How unreasonable is such a callus behavior? Yet, we mimic this wicked servant anytime that we are unwilling to release the offenses of others to the Lord, who has forgiven us of so much more.

God is a forgiving God, but He judges those who willfully trample on His mercy with unthankful and unforgiving hearts. In light of the enormous debt of sin forgiven us through the work of Calvary, let us release to God the lesser ills that we have suffered by others. Bitterness and rejoicing are both choices: The former is a decision to swallow a poison that rots the soul, while the latter choice delights in the character and attributes of our great God, who is always faithful to do good and judge all injustice. To be unforgiving of others is to behave like a wicked servant who is out of touch with the heart of God.

The Good Samaritan

> *And behold, a certain lawyer stood up and tested Him, saying, "Teacher, what shall I do to inherit eternal life?" He said to him, "What is written in the law? What is your reading of it?" So he answered and said, "'You shall love the Lord your God with all your heart, with all your soul, with all your strength, and with all your mind,' and 'your neighbor as yourself.'" And He said to him, "You have answered rightly; do this and you will live."*
>
> *But he, wanting to justify himself, said to Jesus, "And who is my neighbor?" Then Jesus answered and said: "A certain man went down from Jerusalem to Jericho, and fell among thieves, who stripped him of his clothing, wounded him, and departed, leaving him half dead. Now by chance a certain priest came down that road. And when he saw him, he passed by on the other side. Likewise a Levite, when he arrived at the place, came and looked, and passed by on the other side. But a certain Samaritan, as he journeyed, came where he was. And when he saw him, he had compassion. So he went to him and bandaged his wounds, pouring on oil and wine; and he set him on his own animal, brought him to an inn, and took care of him. On the next day, when he departed, he took out two denarii, gave them to the innkeeper, and said to him, 'Take care of him; and whatever more you spend, when I come again, I will repay you.' So which of these three do you think was neighbor to him who fell among the thieves?" And he said, "He who showed mercy on him." Then Jesus said to him, "Go and do likewise"* (Luke 10:25-37).

The parable of *The Good Samaritan* is only found in the Gospel of Luke. The story was spoken to a lawyer during the Lord's Judean Ministry (about six months before Calvary). The text informs us that the lawyer was not truly interested in gaining eternal life, but rather sought an opportunity to test the Lord. Perhaps the lawyer thought he could somehow outwit the Lord Jesus or trip Him up in His words. Regardless of his motivation, the lawyer desired to be justified before others rather than being justified by God.

The Lord answered the lawyer's question about how to inherit eternal life with two of His own: *"What is written in the law?"* and *"What is your reading of it?"* By doing so, the Lord Jesus caused the man to personally consider what the Word of God stated about the matter of salvation. The Lord's response to this insincere inquirer is a good one for us to follow when interacting with the unregenerate: Answer a question with a question which causes the inquirer to examine God's Word (Scripture) for His answer.

Believers today would do well to remember that we are merely facilitators of Scripture; we say no more than what God has commissioned us to speak. The Holy Spirit is the One responsible for working in the hearts of those who hear God's Word. Yet, an individual cannot repent and receive Christ as Savior without first understanding the Word of God, for *"faith comes by hearing, and hearing by the word of God"* (Rom. 10:17).

The lawyer answered the Lord's questions by quoting an appropriate portion of Scripture – to sacrificially love God with your whole being and then to demonstrate that same kind of genuine love to others pleases God. The Lord not only stated that the lawyer's answer was correct, but also applied its meaning – if anyone fully lived in this way, they would be accepted by God. The Lord Jesus would later state that all the tenets of the Law hung on these two commandments – properly loving God and our fellowman (Matt. 22:40). The first four of the Ten Commandments relate to the former idea and the last six to the latter one.

Basically, the Lord affirmed this hypothetical truth, because the lawyer needed to be made aware that he had not fully and perfectly kept the Law. In fact, it was an impossibility that anyone born of Adam could keep the Mosaic Law to please God, because no one could fully keep it. Paul therefore concludes: *"By the deeds of the law no flesh will be justified in His sight, for by the law is the knowledge of sin"* (Rom. 3:20). If the lawyer wanted to approach God through Law-keeping, he would never be justified before God.

The discussion should have ended there, but since the lawyer was eager to promote himself, he quickly asked another question in response to the Lord's concise response to his first inquiry. The Lord spoke the parable of *The Good Samaritan* in response to the lawyer's question, "Who is my neighbor?"

The priest and the Levite in the story had a legitimate opportunity to demonstrate love for the wounded man, their neighbor, but they declined to do so. However, a Samaritan passing by and seeing the injured party was moved with compassion and did his best to ensure his recovery. The robbed man was apparently a Jew, so the act of the Samaritan was especially kind, as ethnic hatred and religious etiquette kept the two people groups apart. The Jews considered the Samaritans as unclean dogs. The Samaritans were a mixed Jewish-Gentile people group which developed in central Israel after the Assyrian invasion of the Northern Kingdom in the eighth century B.C.

The racial hatred of the Jewish lawyer was exhibited after the Lord asked the lawyer who had been a good neighbor to the injured man in the story. The lawyer could not force himself to utter the word "Samaritan" in his response, but rather said "he who had mercy." Regardless of their social abhorrence of the Samaritans, the Jews listening to the Lord's story were all wishing that they could be like the good Samaritan in the parable!

The Lord's response to the lawyer's first question was intended to speak to his conscience: only perfect Law-keepers would have God's approval and receive eternal life. The purpose of the parable was to cause the hearers to look beyond the impossibility of self-justification to being justified through Himself, their Savior. The crux of the story was this point: If the needy man in the story could receive help from a Samaritan, why will you not receive help from Me concerning your dire situation of sin?

The Friend at Midnight and Fatherhood

> *And He said to them, "Which of you shall have a friend, and go to him at midnight and say to him, 'Friend, lend me three loaves; for a friend of mine has come to me on his journey, and I have nothing to set before him'; and he will answer from within and say, 'Do not trouble me; the door is now shut, and my children are with me in bed; I cannot rise and give to you'? I say to you, though he will not rise and give to him because he is his friend, yet because of his persistence he will rise and give him as many as he needs. So I say to you, ask, and it will be given to you; seek, and you will find; knock, and it will be opened to you. For everyone who asks receives, and he who seeks finds, and to him who knocks it will be opened"* (Luke 11:5-8).

This parable was spoken shortly after *The Good Samaritan* parable during the Lord's Judean ministry. The disciples, after observing His intimate prayer-life, wanted to have the same kind of experience with God; hence, they asked, "Lord, teach us to pray." After the Lord shared with them a pattern of prayer to follow (not a prayer to be repeated by rote), He spoke these two parables. Both stories further exemplified important aspects of fruitful prayer-life.

Interestingly, the Lord had already taught them this same model prayer about a year and a half earlier on the Mount of Olives (Matt. 6:9-13). Apparently, after observing the Lord's passionate prayer-life, they still felt deficient in how they were conversing with God.

Both parables convey the idea of persistent praying…asking, seeking, knocking, until the God of heaven provides answers to that which is burdening our hearts (Matt. 7:7). Besides *yes*, *no*, or *different* answers to our prayers, we must realize that our tunnel vision perception of things often inhibits us from waiting for a sovereign God to work out His will in time. It will always be His best for us to wait for what God has for us. As the prophet Habakkuk learned, what often seems to be a *delayed* answer to our prayers is actually a legitimate response of a loving and holy God at work.

We should not think that these parables infer that God is somehow annoyed at our persistent praying or that He will be forced to answer a prayer in a particular way because He has heard it many times. Rather, the idea is that if a reluctant friend will respond to the inconvenient request of his neighbor for three loaves of bread, how much more likely is God to grant our requests. We are not unwelcomed neighbors, for God has invited every believer to come boldly into His presence to receive His help in time of need (Heb. 4:16). We have confidence that if we are praying in the will of God, such prayers will be answered appropriately to honor His name.

Similarly, in the second parable, it is expected and appropriate for a father to feed his children, rather than allowing them to hunger because of neglect. How much more then should we expect our heavenly Father to bestow goodness to His children so that they do not needlessly lack! *"Every good gift and every perfect gift is from above, and comes down from the Father of lights, with whom there is no variation or shadow of turning"* (Jas. 1:17).

We read of the Lord Jesus instructing His disciples seven times in the Gospel of John to pray only in His name. Such prayers are to be founded in God's Word and directed to the Father: *"And whatever you ask in My name, that I will do, that the Father may be glorified in the Son. If you ask anything in My name, I will do it. If you love Me, keep My commandments"* (John 14:13-15). *"Whatever you ask the Father in*

My name He may give you" (John 15:16). If *friendship* caused the hesitant neighbor to supply the requested bread in the parable, how much more will *sonship* prompt the ever-willing Father to supply all our needs in real life?

The Rich Fool

> *Then He spoke a parable to them, saying: "The ground of a certain rich man yielded plentifully. And he thought within himself, saying, 'What shall I do, since I have no room to store my crops?' So he said, 'I will do this: I will pull down my barns and build greater, and there I will store all my crops and my goods. And I will say to my soul, "Soul, you have many goods laid up for many years; take your ease; eat, drink, and be merry."' But God said to him, 'Fool! This night your soul will be required of you; then whose will those things be which you have provided?'" So is he who lays up treasure for himself, and is not rich toward God* (Luke 12:16-21).

This parable was spoken towards the end of the Lord's Judean Ministry, just before the *Feast of Dedication* in December 29 A.D. Instead of sharing the blessings of a bountiful harvest with others, the rich man built more barns in an attempt to hoard for himself what God had entrusted to Him. His needs were amply met, so he could have avoided the unnecessary construction expenses by distributing the excess to those in need. But this was not his choice.

God severely judged the rich man for his poor stewardship – he had used what God had given him to exalt himself and to gain prosperity instead of assisting others. When God supplies beyond our needs, our first recourse should be to discern why, and who He would desire us to bless. The rich man valued temporary wealth over eternal riches; let us not follow his example.

Not only did the rich man lose everything that he valued on earth, but his life was forfeited also. He had expended his time and resources to achieve temporal advancement, but he had gained nothing that counted for eternity. Those who desire to live independently from God ultimately have an existence apart from Him – this is called "death" in Scripture.

What is the application for us today? We are all stewards of what God has given us and we all must give an account to Him; may we all be found faithful on that day (1 Cor. 4:2). Believers should not hoard God's blessings, but rather keep His provisions in circulation so that others can experience the goodness of God also. This describes the spirit of equality that Paul says should exist among God's people (2 Cor. 8:13-14). Our lives must not be defined by what we think we have, but rather by what Christ has that we are to share with others.

Consequently, the Lord followed the parable with an exhortation and a promise to His disciples (Luke 12:22-24). The disciples were not to worry about life's necessities – God would take care of them. Accordingly, they were not to focus their attention on temporal things, but instead on what benefits God's kingdom.

The Ambitious Guest

> *So He told a parable to those who were invited, when He noted how they chose the best places, saying to them: "When you are invited by anyone to a wedding feast, do not sit down in the best place, lest one more honorable than you be invited by him; and he who invited you and him come and say to you, 'Give place to this man,' and then you begin with shame to take the lowest place. But when you are invited, go and sit down in the lowest place, so that when he who invited you comes he may say to you, 'Friend, go up higher.' Then you will have glory in the presence of those who sit at the table with you. For whoever exalts himself will be humbled, and he who humbles himself will be exalted."*
>
> *Then He also said to him who invited Him, "When you give a dinner or a supper, do not ask your friends, your brothers, your relatives, nor rich neighbors, lest they also invite you back, and you be repaid. But when you give a feast, invite the poor, the maimed, the lame, the blind. And you will be blessed, because they cannot repay you; for you shall be repaid at the resurrection of the just"* (Luke 14:7-14).

This parable and the next four were told at nearly the same time during Christ's Perean ministry during the Winter of 29-30 A.D. (beginning about four months before Calvary). The first two stories were told while eating a meal in the house of a Pharisee on the Sabbath day. The latter three parables were spoken to a crowd that was following the Lord while He was walking to His next destination.

A Pharisee had invited the Lord and the esteemed and well-to-do of the community to enjoy a meal at his home. The Lord noticed that the poor and uninfluential were not present, and that those who were attending were seeking to sit in the most honorable seats. He responded to this dynamic by telling the story of *The Ambitious Guest.* Arriving at a wedding feast, the ambitious guest chose an honorable seat, but was later humiliated when asked by the host to sit in a less prominent place because someone more honorable than he had just arrived.

There are two main applications from this parable. First, we should not be respecters of persons. Everyone deserves kindness, but the underprivileged had not been invited to this wedding feast. Second, Paul tells us that those having the mind of Christ do not exalt themselves, but willingly take the low place and elevate the needs of others above their own (Phil. 2:2-5). We are not to follow the example of the ambitious guest in the story. He demonstrated by sitting in the best place at the wedding feast that he thought highly of himself and wanted others to esteem him as being more important than others at the feast. This is not the mind of Christ!

While social etiquette may cause us not to seek an exalted position when in the company of others, the issue that the Lord is addressing goes much deeper than just behavior. It is natural for our carnal flesh to want others to esteem us as important, and we usually feel affronted if that does not happen. For example, how do you feel when you are not recognized by others for an achievement that you labored diligently for? It is also natural for us to minimize others in order to make ourselves feel significant. For example, how do you respond when people treat you like a servant when you have freely shown kindness to them? If we have the mind of Christ (i.e., possess genuine humility), we would not be offended at either situation; in fact, the possibility of being offended would never enter our minds.

Believers may be recognized and honored by others for humble, diligent service, but such accolades should not be sought after. We are only on earth presently for the praise of God's glory (i.e., to make God look good; 1 Cor. 10:31; Eph. 1:12). Genuine service to others is given without thought to one's self or what others may think. This means that if we are grumbling and complaining while serving or hoping that we will be recognized by others for what we are doing, we are not really serving the Lord, but ourselves (Matt. 6:2; Phil. 2:14).

The Great Supper

Now when one of those who sat at the table with Him heard these things, he said to Him, "Blessed is he who shall eat bread in the kingdom of God!"

Then He said to him, "A certain man gave a great supper and invited many, and sent his servant at suppertime to say to those who were invited, 'Come, for all things are now ready.' But they all with one accord began to make excuses. The first said to him, 'I have bought a piece of ground, and I must go and see it. I ask you to have me excused.' And another said, 'I have bought five yoke of oxen, and I am going to test them. I ask you to have me excused.' Still another said, 'I have married a wife, and therefore I cannot come.' So that servant came and reported these things to his master. Then the master of the house, being angry, said to his servant, 'Go out quickly into the streets and lanes of the city, and bring in here the poor and the maimed and the lame and the blind.' And the servant said, 'Master, it is done as you commanded, and still there is room.' Then the master said to the servant, 'Go out into the highways and hedges, and compel them to come in, that my house may be filled. For I say to you that none of those men who were invited shall taste my supper'" (Luke 14:15-24).

The Lord told *The Great Supper* parable to express God's desire for heaven to be full of redeemed sinners, but sadly most will snub His kind offer to feast with Him. A certain man (representing the Lord) sent out his servants (speaking of the disciples) with invitations to a great feast to be held at his home. The invites went to *the many* (i.e., Jewish leaders), to *the people in the streets* (i.e., common Jews), to *the people on the highways* traveling through the land (i.e., the Gentiles), and lastly to anyone in need (picturing the poor, the blind, the crippled, the lame, etc.).

Many made excuses for not attending the great feast. Only a wealthy person buys property before looking at it first. Materialism and wealth, speaking of self-sufficiency, are often a hindrance for considering the gospel message of Christ. The excuse of testing five yoke of oxen just purchased pictures how jobs, careers, and business affairs often impede people from heeding Christ's invitation. A husband spending time with his new wife would be a proper expectation, but no natural relationships should keep us from seeking the only One who will satisfy the longing in our souls – Christ.

After hearing *The Great Supper* parable, a crowd began following Christ, but knowing that many just desired a good meal and not spiritual transformation, He stopped and turned towards them, and taught them about the cost of following Him. The Lord was much more interested in the commitment of His disciples to Him than in the crowd of people merely following Him. The Lord desired disciples who would learn of Him and be loyal to Him without reservation.

In secular movements, numbers are everything, but rarely do vast hordes of people represent God's will. This anomaly is quite evident in the modern Church movement, which equates church attendance with success. The mindset is that big church meetings are obviously evidence of divine blessing. However, it is making true disciples of Christ that is the key to Church growth and vitality (Matt. 28:19-20). May we too heed the command to "go out quickly" with the gospel message and compel anyone who will listen to consider God's offer in Christ. The various gimmicks used today in Churchianity to get the unregenerate into their buildings are a poor substitute for the message of Christ. May believers remember that what we win people with is what we win them to. Ultimately, any message that steps around the gospel of Jesus Christ to gain followers will leave hungry souls dissatisfied and yearning for that which is better.

The response to *The Great Supper* parable also shows us that just because a large group of people gather after the name of Christ does not mean that they are legitimate followers. The Lord longs for the genuine disciples and both Church history and biblical history indicate that a religious majority has rarely aligned with God. Rather, crowds normally embrace doctrinal compromise and shallow spirituality, while a mere "remnant" comprise the real thing (Hag. 1:12-14; Rom. 9:27, 11:5).

The Lord Jesus demonstrated by His choice and order of parables in Luke 14 that, in spiritual matters, the mainstream rarely has God's interests at heart. The Lord was not interested in the quantity, but in the quality of those following Him. The next three parables emphasize this point – true discipleship is an all-or-nothing proposition.

The Unfinished Tower, the King's Rash War, and Salt

> *Now great multitudes went with Him. And He turned and said to them, "If anyone comes to Me and does not hate his father and mother, wife and children, brothers and sisters, yes, and his own life also, he cannot be My disciple. And whoever does not bear his cross and come after Me cannot be My disciple. For which of you, intending to build a tower, does not sit down first and count the cost, whether he has enough to finish it – lest, after he has laid the foundation, and is not able to finish, all who see it begin to mock him, saying, 'This man began to build and was not able to finish.' Or what king, going to make war against another king, does not sit down first and consider whether he is able with ten thousand to meet him who comes against him with twenty thousand? Or else, while the other is still a great way off, he sends a delegation and asks conditions of peace. So likewise, whoever of you does not forsake all that he has cannot be My disciple."*
>
> *"Salt is good; but if the salt has lost its flavor, how shall it be seasoned? It is neither fit for the land nor for the dunghill, but men throw it out. He who has ears to hear, let him hear!"* (Luke 14:25-33).

These three parables were told together and have a common message – to follow Christ is an all-or-nothing venture. It is foolish to begin building a tower, without first assuring that one has the resources in place to finish it. If started and abandoned because of poor planning at the onset, the builder will lose the initial investment and appear foolish to others. Likewise, if a king decides to take on an invasion force twice the size of his own army, it must be an all-out effort – any haphazard effort will end in defeat. He and his soldiers must give their all in the defense of their city or capitulate and offer terms of surrender to avoid the battle.

Salt adds flavor to what is eaten, and also serves as a food preservative. But if salt loses its flavor and seasoning ability, it is worthless and must be discarded. Paul used salt as a metaphor to speak of uncompromised truth (Col. 4:6). Salt, then, stands in contrast with leaven, which corrupts. This is why the Lord Jesus exhorts His disciples to have a "salty" testimony (also see Matt. 5:13). In summary, a disciple of Christ must display uncompromised truth while living in total dedication to Christ.

Our desire to follow Christ is a measure of how much we truly love Him and believe His message. The reason we hold back from being fools for Christ, and thus from seeing the mighty hand of God in our lives, is disbelief – we don't trust God. Through disbelief, the One who was offended for us becomes an offense to us. Those associating with Christ superficially will ultimately find Him offensive. The Lord Jesus didn't teach a middle ground concerning discipleship; those who follow Him were to do so without any reservation:

> *If anyone desires to come after Me, let him deny himself, and take up his cross daily, and follow Me. For whoever desires to save his life will lose it, but whoever loses his life for My sake will save it* (Luke 9:23-34).
>
> *If anyone comes to Me and does not hate his father and mother, wife and children, brothers and sisters, yes, and his own life also, he cannot be My disciple* (Luke 14:26).
>
> *And whoever does not bear his cross and come after Me cannot be My disciple* (Luke 14:27).
>
> *So likewise, whoever of you does not forsake all that he has cannot be My disciple* (Luke 14:33).

The Lord never spoke of "becoming" His disciple, but what it meant to "be" His disciple, which implies an active, ongoing commitment. Consequently, He tells us not to call Him Lord, if we are not willing to do what He commands (Luke 6:46). He must be Lord of all, or He is not Lord at all. Christianity is more than coming to the Lord for salvation; it is also going on with Him to live out His spiritual life before others. We come to His cross and leave with our own cross. The cross is a symbol of shame and death, and Christ asks those who believe in Him to follow His selfless example of faithfulness, even unto death. On the night before His crucifixion, the Lord told His disciples that by identifying with Him, they would experience the world's hatred and persecution (John 15:18-20).

The gospel message pleads for the hell-bound sinner to embrace the cross of Christ, and no less so for the heaven-bound saint to take up his or her cross that he or she might enjoy life now. The Lord does not want us to only believe upon Him to evade judgment; He wants us to become like Him through exercising obedient faith. If we truly believe the gospel message, we will yield to Him and experience His abundant life now (John 10:10). We validate what we believe by what we do!

The Lost Sheep

> *Then all the tax collectors and the sinners drew near to Him to hear Him. And the Pharisees and scribes complained, saying, "This Man receives sinners and eats with them." So He spoke this parable to them, saying: "What man of you, having a hundred sheep, if he loses one of them, does not leave the ninety-nine in the wilderness, and go after the one which is lost until he finds it? And when he has found it, he lays it on his shoulders, rejoicing. And when he comes home, he calls together his friends and neighbors, saying to them, 'Rejoice with me, for I have found my sheep which was lost!' I say to you that likewise there will be more joy in heaven over one sinner who repents than over ninety-nine just persons who need no repentance"* (Luke 15:1-7).

The parables of three lost things were spoken together by the Lord during His Perean ministry to pose a singular and crucial message to His audience. It is noteworthy that the Lord Jesus is addressing a mixed audience of those interested in listening to His message and those who were already rejecting it. Apparently, those seeking to be found were positioned near to the Lord, while the murmuring religious leaders kept their distance. Yet, they were still close enough to hear the stories, and, in fact, the parable trilogy had been crafted for their benefit.

The Lord begins by telling of one sheep that wandered away from the flock and the protection of the shepherd. The shepherd, not willing to lose any of his sheep, left the ninety-nine to find the one missing. The lost sheep is likened to foolish sinners who wander aimlessly pursuing their own cravings, but are never satisfied. When a lost soul comes to the end of himself or herself, a seeking Savior will be right there to pick them up and carry them home on His shoulders. The Lord notes that there is great joy in heaven when one soul repents and receives deliverance through God's divine Shepherd – Christ.

No doubt, as the Pharisees considered the parable, they considered themselves as the ninety-nine good sheep who were not lost, and they were correct in their assessment! The ninety-nine sheep represented the self-righteous who did not need to repent because they were good Law-keepers.

The Lost Coin

> *"Or what woman, having ten silver coins, if she loses one coin, does not light a lamp, sweep the house, and search carefully until she finds it? And when she has found it, she calls her friends and neighbors together, saying, 'Rejoice with me, for I have found the piece which I lost!' Likewise, I say to you, there is joy in the presence of the angels of God over one sinner who repents"* (Luke 15:8-10).

In the second parable of the series, *The Lost Coin*, the Lord narrows the focus on the Pharisees further by decreasing the ratio from 99:1 to 9:1. It was customary for a married Jewish woman to keep part of her marriage dowry, ten silver coins, in her headdress in the event that she might be suddenly handed a bill of divorce. In this heart-breaking situation, the divorced wife was often put out on the street with only what she was wearing, so the silver coins in her headdress would be used to sustain herself until friends or family could assist her. All this to say that losing one of these ten silver coins was a serious matter, so with a lighted lamp, the woman would sweep the entire house looking for what was lost. As with the lost sheep that was found, the recovered lost coin represents a sinner's repentance which again caused rejoicing in heaven.

Whereas the sheep was lost through craving-driven wandering, the coin was lost through carelessness. A coin bears the image of the one in authority, and man was created in God's image and likeness. Humanity was to represent God's authority on earth, but all was lost in Eden through satanic deception and human rebellion. God keenly feels the loss of what He created in His own image, so when sinners repent, there is great joy in the presence of the holy angels. Just as the lost coin has value again in the finder's hand, we only have value to God through repentance and being restored to Him through Christ (John 10:28-29).

The Pharisees believed that they were the nine secure coins, who had not been carelessly lost, and they were correct in their thinking. As with the ninety-nine sheep, the nine coins represent the self-righteous who do not need to repent of anything. The Pharisees believed that they were in good standing with God because of their careful attention to Law-keeping.

The Lost Son

Then He said: "A certain man had two sons. And the younger of them said to his father, 'Father, give me the portion of goods that falls to me.' So he divided to them his livelihood. And not many days after, the younger son gathered all together, journeyed to a far country, and there wasted his possessions with prodigal living. But when he had spent all, there arose a severe famine in that land, and he began to be in want. Then he went and joined himself to a citizen of that country, and he sent him into his fields to feed swine. And he would gladly have filled his stomach with the pods that the swine ate, and no one gave him anything.

"But when he came to himself, he said, 'How many of my father's hired servants have bread enough and to spare, and I perish with hunger! I will arise and go to my father, and will say to him, "Father, I have sinned against heaven and before you, and I am no longer worthy to be called your son. Make me like one of your hired servants."'"

"And he arose and came to his father. But when he was still a great way off, his father saw him and had compassion, and ran and fell on his neck and kissed him. And the son said to him, 'Father, I have sinned against heaven and in your sight, and am no longer worthy to be called your son.' But the father said to his servants, 'Bring out the best robe and put it on him, and put a ring on his hand and sandals on his feet. And bring the fatted calf here and kill it, and let us eat and be merry; for this my son was dead and is alive again; he was lost and is found.' And they began to be merry."

"Now his older son was in the field. And as he came and drew near to the house, he heard music and dancing. So he called one of the servants and asked what these things meant. And he said to him, 'Your brother has come, and because he has received him safe and sound, your father has killed the fatted calf.' But he was angry and would not go in. Therefore his father came out and pleaded with him. So he answered and said to his father, 'Lo, these many years I have been serving you; I never transgressed your commandment at any time; and yet you never gave me a young goat, that I might make

> *merry with my friends. But as soon as this son of yours came, who has devoured your livelihood with harlots, you killed the fatted calf for him.'"*
>
> *"And he said to him, 'Son, you are always with me, and all that I have is yours. It was right that we should make merry and be glad, for your brother was dead and is alive again, and was lost and is found'"* (Luke 15:11-32).

The Lord again decreased the ratio of the self-righteous souls in correlation to lost sinners coming to repentance from 9:1 to 1:1. The Lord's illustration is narrowing in on the hard-hearted, religious zealots who felt they were accepted by God without repenting of their sins.

In the story, a wealthy man has two sons. The older son is compliant, but the younger son comes to the point of wanting his inheritance before His father died. He desired to live his life the way he wanted to and that meant not being under his father's authority. This was an especially hurtful request to the father who loved his son. First, it suggested that the younger son wished that his father was dead. Second, the younger son thought that he would be much happier having no contact with his father. Regardless, the father granted his son's request and having received his inheritance went to a far country and squandered all that he had on riotous activities.

When the prodigal son's money was spent, his supposed friends abandoned him. His dire situation was compounded by a famine in the land which made finding work difficult, but at last he found a job feeding swine. A Jew could stoop no lower than this occupation, as swine were unclean animals under the Law. The prodigal son became so hunger that he even thought about eating the slop he was feeding the swine. It was then that he came to himself. He decided that it would be far better for him to return to his father, confess his sin, and just be as a servant in his father's house.

Apparently, day after day, the father searched the horizon for his wayward son, and one day, he spotted his son at a distance coming towards him. The father ran to meet his son and immediately embraced him and kissed him. The son confessed his sin to his father, but he was never permitted to offer his service as a slave, for the father joyfully restored him to the status of his son. The returning son was given the best robe to wear, a ring for his hand, and sandals for his feet.

Additionally, the father had the fatted calf slaughtered and prepared for a great feast.

There was much joy and festivity in the father's house that day, for the son that was dead and lost had been found and made alive again! After experiencing such sincere love and care that day, there can be little doubt that the younger son wondered why he had ever forsaken his father. It did not matter that he had broken his father's heart, had wasted his money, and had engaged in wanton behavior, nor that he was filthy and smelled like swine; his father, delighted to see him, hugged and kissed him anyway.

The Pharisees readily aligned with the compliant older son who did not desert the father or engage in depraved acts and again they were correct in their assessment. But as the story continues, we will find out that though the older son was near to the father, he was just as lost as the younger son.

The older son had been working in a field, but as he neared his father's house, he could hear the sounds of music and merrymaking and inquired what all the hoopla was about. He became angry after learning that his troublesome younger brother had returned home and had been well received. In fact, the entire party was in his honor.

It is when the father comes out to speak to his older son that we discover the wrong disposition of his heart. The older son bemoaned that he had always been loyal to his father, but had never been given a kid of the goats so he could feast with his friends. Yet, his father had prepared the fatted calf for his disloyal son who returned home after squandering his livelihood on frivolous and lascivious activities.

Previously, the father departed from his place to seek and welcome his prodigal son home. Now, the father went to do the same with the older son, who was near the house. But the older son would not venture through the same door of repentance as the younger son had, even though the father begged him to do so. The older son, who had been attempting to please his father by doing good works, could not accept the same love of the father that had forgiven his younger son. The older son looked good on the outside, but was just as lost. He disdains his father's younger son because of the grace that he had received from the father. It is for this reason that he never refers to him as "his brother," for how could he be? Only those who have experienced salvation in Christ can be call "brethren."

The Jews had the Law, which meant that they were closer to God than those without the Law, but since no one could keep the Law perfectly, even the most pious religious leaders must also humble themselves through repentance to be welcomed into God's family and dwelling place. Whether residing in a far country or in a field near the father's house, both brothers were just as lost.

Even though the father begged the older son to come into his house, he would not. The older son here represents the religious Jews that were listening to the parable. They would have readily identified themselves with the older son in the parable and they were correct. The older son boasted of his good works for the father, but he had not yet experienced the father's love, as the repentant younger son had. The Pharisees would not enter the same door of repentance as the younger son, and, hence, they were just as lost as the most wicked sinner wandering aimlessly far away from God.

The Second Coming and Jewish Attitudes

Parable Title	Reference
The Rude Children	Luke 7:31-35
The Barren Fig Tree	Luke 13:6-9
The Unjust Judge	Luke 18:1-8
The Pharisee & the Tax Collector	Luke 18:9-14
The Two Sons	Matt. 21:28-32
The Landowner & Vinedressers	Matt. 21:33-46; Mark 12:1-12; Lk. 20:9-19
The Marriage Feast	Matt. 22:1-14
The Ten Virgins	Matt. 25:1-13
The Door Keeper	Mark 13:34-37

The remaining parables to consider largely focus on the Lord's second coming and were mainly told in the final few months of His earthly ministry. The parables contained in this chapter were spoken to confront religious pride and foretell the consequences of the Jewish rejection of Christ.

The Rude Children

> *And the Lord said, "To what then shall I liken the men of this generation, and what are they like? They are like children sitting in the marketplace and calling to one another, saying: 'We played the flute for you, and you did not dance; we mourned to you, and you did not weep.' For John the Baptist came neither eating bread nor drinking wine, and you say, 'He has a demon.' The Son of Man has come eating and drinking, and you say, 'Look, a glutton and a winebibber, a friend of tax collectors and sinners!' But wisdom is justified by all her children"* (Luke 7:31-35).

This parable was spoken shortly after the *Sermon on the Mount* address in the Galilean Ministry (probably late Spring 28 A.D.). While the Pharisees held the respect of the people, they did not have God's favor. They were self-exalting and self-focused; they measured the spirituality of others by their own standards of religiosity.

The Lord likened the Pharisees to children in the street dancing to their own piped songs. William MacDonald writes:

> They didn't want to play either wedding or funeral. They were perverse, wayward, unpredictable, and refractory. No matter what ministry God used among them, they took exception to it.[9]

Anyone who did not join their religious escapades was rejected by them. For example, John the Baptizer lived a simple existence in the wilderness while he fulfilled his ministry. Additionally, the Pharisees accused the Lord of extravagant living because He ate and drank with those He came to save. Neither John's near impoverished lifestyle in the wilderness while calling sinners to repentance nor the Lord's compassionate efforts to awaken the wealthy of their spiritual need had their approval.

Religious moralizers will attack those faithfully declaring God's Word in whatever way they can to avoid considering what God wants them to hear. The Old Testament prophets repeatedly suffered this type of abuse and at times were imprisoned or put to death to suppress their preaching. Clearly, those who live for the Lord will never be able to please the Pharisaical mentality. Whether today or in Christ's day, Pharisees danced only to their own music! Israel's religious leaders had lulled themselves into a self-absorbed existence that resulted in willful complacency of the things important to God, especially the care of His people.

Thankfully, the Lord Jesus was not distracted by their criticism or by their rejection of His message. Rather, He ignored their opposition and kept to the work that God gave Him to accomplish. When faced with pharisaical pride, this is a good example for us to follow also. If you are faithfully serving the Lord in your divine calling, you will be criticized; so, expect it. Benefit from what is profitable, and forget what is not, but keep serving the Lord regardless. If the devil can get us defending ourselves against unjust criticism – he gains the victory over us. Satan gains a victory when he pulls us out of God's work into his own wicked agenda!

The Barren Fig Tree

> *He also spoke this parable: "A certain man had a fig tree planted in his vineyard, and he came seeking fruit on it and found none. Then he said to the keeper of his vineyard, 'Look, for three years I have come seeking fruit on this fig tree and find none. Cut it down; why does it use up the ground?' But he answered and said to him, 'Sir, let it alone this year also, until I dig around it and fertilize it. And if it bears fruit, well. But if not, after that you can cut it down'"* (Luke 13:6-9).

Christ spoke this parable just before the Feast of Dedication and at the conclusion of His Judean ministry in the Fall of 29 A.D.

The Jewish nation is allegorically likened to a foliage trilogy in Scripture: the vine, the fig tree, and the olive tree. Each one represents a distinct aspect of Israel's existence. The nation of Israel, as a political reality, is likened to a noble vine (a grape vine; Jer. 8:13), which God planted in the world (Jer. 2:21, 12:10); Israel was to be God's vineyard.

At the end of the Tribulation Period, the refined Jewish nation will receive the Holy Spirit and obtain spiritual life in Christ (Zech. 12:10). The work of the Holy Spirit in Israel is similarly depicted by the oil flowing to a lampstand from the olive tree in Zechariah's vision (Zech. 4:4-7). In this spiritually fruitful state, the Jews will be known as the olive tree which provides a testimony of God's goodness to the entire world (Hos. 14:6; Rom. 11:17-24).

When Israel is spoken of as a fig tree in Scripture, the metaphor relates to Israel's religious veracity, which often was fruitless for God (Jer. 8:13). This reality, including Judaism today, is what the Lord Jesus is addressing in this parable. After preaching the Kingdom message for three-plus years to the lost sheep of Israel, Christ cursed the fruitless fig tree just before His death at Calvary (Matt. 21:18-21). He sought spiritual fruit from the nation of Israel and none was found. Less than forty years later, Jerusalem and the temple were destroyed and the Jews have not sacrificed since that time. The Old Covenant was replaced by the New Covenant, sealed with Christ's blood, and God was determined not to allow the Jews to continue in what was now obsolete (Heb. 8:8-13).

One of the signs that the Tribulation Period and the Second Advent of Christ are nearing is that the fig tree (i.e., religious Israel) will again shoot forth leaves after a long winter season of deadness (Luke 21:29-31). Leaves must precede fruit, but the fig tree will bear no fruit until the spiritual rebirth of the nation occurs in the latter days of the Tribulation Period. What might the new leaves speak of? This is likely a reference to the Jews reviving the old sacrificial system during, and perhaps just prior to, the Tribulation Period.

We know from various prophecies that the Antichrist will desecrate the Jewish temple and put a stop to animal sacrifices at the midpoint of the Tribulation Period (Dan. 9:27; Matt. 24:15; 2 Thess. 2:3-7). Therefore, logically speaking, a temple will have to be erected and animal sacrifices will have to be reinstituted by that point. The generation that sees these activities will certainly see the coming of the Lord Jesus in His glory (Matt. 24:32-35). But presently, the fig tree, Israel's religious system, is leaf-less (i.e., no animal sacrifices) and fruitless (void of spiritual vitality).

The Unjust Judge

> *Then He spoke a parable to them, that men always ought to pray and not lose heart, saying: "There was in a certain city a judge who did not fear God nor regard man. Now there was a widow in that city; and she came to him, saying, 'Get justice for me from my adversary.' And he would not for a while; but afterward he said within himself, 'Though I do not fear God nor regard man, yet because this widow troubles me I will avenge her, lest by her continual coming she weary me.'"*
>
> *Then the Lord said, "Hear what the unjust judge said. And shall God not avenge His own elect who cry out day and night to Him, though He bears long with them? I tell you that He will avenge them speedily. Nevertheless, when the Son of Man comes, will He really find faith on the earth?"* (Luke 18:1-8).

The parable was apparently told just after Christ raised Lazarus from the dead, but just prior to his final journey to Jerusalem. Though this parable was told during the Lord's Perean ministry, the location at which it was uttered may have been in Samaria.

The unrighteous judge in the story did not fear God. He also was not motivated by the factual evidence of the case to issue a proper ruling against the widow's oppressor. Furthermore, the magistrate displayed no compassion for her plight. So why did the unjust, atheistic, cold-hearted judge finally rule in the widow's favor? The answer is, because of her persistent pleading.

The point of the parable is this: If the unrighteous, unsympathetic judge will rule on the behalf of the widow, how much more willing will God the Father, who is righteous and caring, be to act in favor of His suffering children. Given the context of the passage, the specific group being spoken of may be the Tribulation saints, but certainly, God desires to abundantly care for all His people in any age.

The idea is that we do not force God to give us what we want because we petition Him often. Rather, we plead with Him often in prayer because we realize that He is our only hope in any hardship. The widow had no one else to turn to for help and neither do we. We trust our Heavenly Father to sustain us through sorrowful times and that He will bring good out of our suffering for His honor and glory (1 Cor. 10:13).

The Pharisee and the Tax Collector

> *Also He spoke this parable to some who trusted in themselves that they were righteous, and despised others: "Two men went up to the temple to pray, one a Pharisee and the other a tax collector. The Pharisee stood and prayed thus with himself, 'God, I thank You that I am not like other men—extortioners, unjust, adulterers, or even as this tax collector. I fast twice a week; I give tithes of all that I possess.' And the tax collector, standing afar off, would not so much as raise his eyes to heaven, but beat his breast, saying, 'God, be merciful to me a sinner!' I tell you, this man went down to his house justified rather than the other; for everyone who exalts himself will be humbled, and he who humbles himself will be exalted"* (Luke 18:9-14).

The Lord was speaking directly to the Pharisees when He uttered this parable. It was spoken just after the *Unjust Judge* parable. The Lord included a Pharisee in His story to confront the proud, self-justifying attitude that characterized many religious leaders at that time. They arrogantly elevated their own spiritual eminence before God by comparing their devout status and pious deeds to those from the general populace. In their minds, they were closer to God because they were spiritually superior to those beneath them, and thus, far more deserving of God's favor. But they were wrong; God is not impressed with a religious facade, but rather assists those who exhibit genuine brokenness, humility, submission, and repentance.

Indeed, the Pharisee in the story prayed and did good deeds, but not to or for God. He prayed to be heard, to be appreciated, and to be honored by others. Previously the Lord warned His audience, *"Therefore, when you do a charitable deed, do not sound a trumpet before you as the hypocrites do in the synagogues and in the streets, that they may have glory from men. Assuredly, I say to you, they have their reward"* (Matt. 6:2). The frequent occurrence of the pronoun "I" in the Pharisee's prayer is indicative of someone suffering from self-sufficiency and pride.

The Pharisee engaged in two prayer activities that should never mark the believers' petitions to a holy God: First, we should not boast to God about what we have done for Him. He knows what we have done, the value of it, and what motivated us to do it. When considering the tremendous cost of our salvation at Calvary, all that we do for God is nothing more than our duty to Him as His redeemed people (Luke 17:10).

Second, we should not boast to God about our spiritual fortitude. This is especially offensive to God when we seek to establish our own spiritual supremacy by comparing ourselves to others. As Paul confirms, anyone with such an attitude will receive God's condemnation (Rom. 2:1-4). God is an omniscient and just Judge. He holds humanity accountable to His standard of righteous (i.e., perfection). Naturally speaking, we all fall short of moral perfection (Rom. 3:23). It is only through being justified in Christ that anyone can be accepted by a holy God into heaven (Rom. 4:2-4). In Christ, we have a positional perfection that can never be lost. Consequently, no one has anything to brag about before God. Paul knew his flesh was biased, so he was hesitant to even judge the value of his own ministry (1 Cor. 4:3-4).

The tax collector exhibits the type of prayer that God appreciates: a spirit of honesty, self-defamation, and humility culminating in genuine repentance. The tax collector did not exalt himself before God, but rather pleaded for mercy, which he received. Ironically, the self-justified Pharisee had the honor of men and the condemnation of God, but the self-defacing tax collector, though disdained by men, was justified by God.

The Two Sons

> *"But what do you think? A man had two sons, and he came to the first and said, 'Son, go, work today in my vineyard.' He answered and said, 'I will not,' but afterward he regretted it and went. Then he came to the second and said likewise. And he answered and said, 'I go, sir,' but he did not go. Which of the two did the will of his father?" They said to Him, "The first."*
>
> *Jesus said to them, "Assuredly, I say to you that tax collectors and harlots enter the kingdom of God before you. For John came to you in the way of righteousness, and you did not believe him; but tax collectors and harlots believed him; and when you saw it, you did not afterward relent and believe him"* (Matt. 21:28-32)

This is the first of three parables spoken together in the temple on the Tuesday before Christ's Crucifixion. The clarity of content and directness of focus in the Lord's final parables is noteworthy.

It is suggested that the first son represents the overall disposition of the Gentiles in Scripture. The opening chapters of Genesis record that the nations were rebellious from the beginning. The rebel behavior of Cain's descendants (Gen. 4), the vast wickedness of humanity during Noah's Day (Gen. 6), and the widespread rebellion of Nimrod at Babel (Gen. 10) all show the disobedient nature of the nations from the beginning.

However, as Hosea prophesied long ago, God would ultimately find a way to call those who were "not His people" – "His people" (Hos. 2:23). Paul explains that this prophecy was fulfilled in the Church Age, when Christ sought a Gentile Bride, the Church, for Himself (Rom. 9:25-26; Eph. 5:25-30). Through repentance and regeneration, Gentiles have become one with Christ and are now obedient to His will.

In contrast, the second son in the parable said that he would labor for his father, but then did not go into the field as he had promised to do. The second son represents the Jewish nation. After being delivered from slavery in Egypt, Israel entered into a covenant with God at Mount Sinai. The Jews promised to do all that God had requested of them in His Law: *"All that the Lord has spoken we will do"* (Ex. 19:8). Yet, only a few days later they were dancing around and revering a golden calf that Aaron had crafted. This was in direct disobedience to the first two of the Ten Commandments.

This unfaithfulness to Jehovah was characteristic of the Jewish people throughout most of the Old Testament record. This same rebel spirit was alive and well in Israel in Christ's day also. Therefore, the Lord rebuked the religious leaders; they were the unfaithful second son. What they said they would do and what they taught others to do, they did not do themselves (Rom. 2:21-23). They were hypocrites of the worst kind because they had the most revelation of what God wanted from them, but they had ignored His Law. Through the parable, Christ was indicating that the Pharisees were being disobedient, unrepentant, unbelieving, and thus dead in their sins.

The Landowner and the Wicked Vinedressers

> *And He said to them ... "Hear another parable: There was a certain landowner who planted a vineyard and set a hedge around it, dug a winepress in it and built a tower. And he leased it to vinedressers and went into a far country. Now when vintage-time drew near, he sent his servants to the vinedressers, that they might receive its fruit. And the vinedressers took his servants, beat one, killed one, and stoned another. Again he sent other servants, more than the first, and they did likewise to them. Then last of all he sent his son to them, saying, 'They will respect my son.' But when the vinedressers saw the son, they said among themselves, 'This is the heir. Come, let us kill him and seize his inheritance.' So they took him and cast him out of the vineyard and killed him."*
>
> *"Therefore, when the owner of the vineyard comes, what will he do to those vinedressers?" They said to Him, "He will destroy those wicked men miserably, and lease his vineyard to other vinedressers who will render to him the fruits in their seasons."*
>
> *Jesus said to them, "Have you never read in the Scriptures: 'The stone which the builders rejected has become the chief cornerstone. This was the Lord's doing, and it is marvelous in our eyes'? Therefore I say to you, the kingdom of God will be taken from you and given to a nation bearing the fruits of it. And whoever falls on this stone will be broken; but on whomever it falls, it will grind him to powder."*

> *Now when the chief priests and Pharisees heard His parables, they perceived that He was speaking of them. But when they sought to lay hands on Him, they feared the multitudes, because they took Him for a prophet* (Matt. 21:27, 33-46).

This is the second of three parables spoken together in the temple on the Tuesday before Christ's Crucifixion. The nation of Israel, as a political reality, is likened to a noble vine (a grape vine; Jer. 8:13), which God planted in the world (Jer. 2:21, 12:10). In fact, several Old Testament prophets refer to Israel as God's special vine that He had planted (e.g., Isa. 5:1-7; Ezek. 15:2-4).

The prophet Hosea rebuked Israel because, though it (as a vine) had lush foliage, its fruit was worthless because it was self-produced for itself, and was not from God or for God: *"Israel empties his vine; he brings forth fruit for himself"* (Hos. 10:1). Two centuries later, the prophet Jeremiah told his fellow countrymen that God had planted a beautiful vineyard (speaking of the Jewish nation), but Israel's shepherds had made it desolate (Jer. 12:10). Israel was God's vineyard, but even in Christ's day, because of spiritually corrupt leaders, it was still not fruitful to God.

God repeatedly attempted to restore the vine to a fruitful condition by sending prophets to rebuke Israel's wayward and carnal leaders, but to no avail. Finally, God sent His beloved Son to plead with Israel to repent and be restored to God, but the Jewish nation rejected Him and had Him put to death. As Paul explains to the Ephesians, the offer of grace in Christ has been presented to the Gentiles who through faith have been brought into the commonwealth of blessing promised to Israel (Eph. 3:2-12). Gentile believers in the "dispensation of the grace of God" (Eph. 3:2) are now bearing spiritual fruit to God. This is what God wanted from Israel, but having rejected Christ, the opportunity was given to those who were not God's covenant people (Rom. 9:25).

The key components of this parable are as follows:

> The certain landowner = God.
>
> The vineyard = Israel.
>
> The vinedressers via lease = Israel's leaders.
>
> The servants = the former prophets and John the Baptizer.

The Son = the Lord Jesus.

The other vinedressers = Gentiles trusting Christ in the Church Age.

Paul's analogy of the olive tree in Romans 11 parallels Christ's teaching in this parable. In this analogy, the root of the tree is the Abrahamic covenant and the olive tree is Christ, through Him the promises of God will bless Israel, the natural branches. Yet, disbelief leads to rebellion and the loss of God's blessings and fellowship. Willful sin and rebellion will always invoke God's chastening hand. God did to Israel exactly what He told them He would do if His people erred from the Law and abandoned Him (Deut. 28); thus, the natural branches (the Jewish people) were removed from the opportunity to be nationally blessed by God through Christ.

Yet, the analogy shows us that God will restore Israel to Himself. The fact that the Jews (the natural branches) could be, and indeed will be, grafted back into the olive tree indicates that the focus of the illustration is not eternal salvation per se, but rather the blessings that God desires to share with those who exercise faith in Him. Gentile believers (the wild branch) are a second benefactor of the New Covenant and thus are permitted to share in the blessings promised Israel (Eph. 2:11-3:7). Gentiles are grafted into the olive tree, indicating the blessings of Christ rooted in God's covenant with Abraham. The New Covenant permits individual Jews to be saved now and the Jewish nation to be reconciled to God after the Church Age ends.

However, when Christ spoke this parable, proud Israel was in rebellion against God, His prophets and His Son, whom they put to death. The tenants wanted the inheritance (to control the people and receive their honor and praise) instead of giving it to the rightful owner – God. The scribes and Pharisees condemned themselves when they declared that the tenants should be killed for their brutal insolence.

After answering Christ's question correctly, the Lord quoted Psalm 118:22 to affirm that God would provide the Gentiles an opportunity to be tenants of His vineyard in order to receive the desired fruit He longed for. At that time, the Jewish nation had no place for Christ; He was the rejected Stone that God then used as a cornerstone to create the Church (i.e., a Gentile bride for His Son). Those who truly repent and receive Christ alone for salvation (i.e., become broken on the Stone) will be saved and have the opportunity to be fruitful to God. But those who reject Christ will be eternally judged by Christ (i.e., crushed to powder by the Stone).

The scribes and Pharisees were infuriated by this conclusion because it was obvious that Christ was likening them to the proud, murderous tenants who would be destroyed. These religious leaders would have arrested the Lord Jesus, but declined to do so for fear of how the crowds listening to Him might respond.

Although the Roman historian Tacitus stated that Jerusalem's population was 600,000 when Rome assaulted the city in 70 A.D., this number seems high as compared with archeological information relating to that timeframe. Examining this evidence, Geva offers a minimal estimate of the city's population to be 20,000 at this time.[10] Others, such as Wikinson[11] and Broshi,[12] put the population of Jerusalem in 70 A.D. to be between 70,000 and 80,000 persons. Though estimates vary, it seems likely that Jerusalem's population at the time of Christ's crucifixion was likely between 50,000 and 80,000 people. However, during religious festivals this number often increased three- to fourfold.

Pilate and the Jewish leaders knew the possibility of social unrest was high at such times and even a riot was a distinct possibility. Hence, because the Pharisees feared the people, they did not arrest the Lord Jesus.

The Marriage Feast

And Jesus answered and spoke to them again by parables and said: "The kingdom of heaven is like a certain king who arranged a marriage for his son, and sent out his servants to call those who were invited to the wedding; and they were not willing to come. Again, he sent out other servants, saying, 'Tell those who are invited, "See, I have prepared my dinner; my oxen and fatted cattle are killed, and all things are ready. Come to the wedding."' But they made light of it and went their ways, one to his own farm, another to his business. And the rest seized his servants, treated them spitefully, and killed them. But when the king heard about it, he was furious. And he sent out his armies, destroyed those murderers, and burned up their city. Then he said to his servants, 'The wedding is ready, but those who were invited were not worthy. Therefore go into the highways, and as many as you find, invite to the wedding.' So those servants went out

> *into the highways and gathered together all whom they found, both bad and good. And the wedding hall was filled with guests."*
>
> *"But when the king came in to see the guests, he saw a man there who did not have on a wedding garment. So he said to him, 'Friend, how did you come in here without a wedding garment?' And he was speechless. Then the king said to the servants, 'Bind him hand and foot, take him away, and cast him into outer darkness; there will be weeping and gnashing of teeth.' For many are called, but few are chosen."* (Matt. 22:1-14).

This parable was spoken to a crowd in Jerusalem directly after the parable of *The Landowner and Wicked Vinedressers* on the Tuesday before Calvary. The Jewish religious leaders were enraged after hearing the previous parable and would have arrested the Lord Jesus, but they feared the reaction of the multitude that was gathering for the Passover.

It is observed that both Matthew and Luke record this parable, but Matthew upholds his authority theme in his account, while Luke punctuates Christ's humanity. Accordingly, Luke refers to the prominent character as *"a certain man"* (Luke 14:16), whereas Matthew is more specific: *"a certain King"* (Matt. 22:2). Both accounts were accurate but different. Matthew upholds the kingly assertion of Christ in his Gospel, while Luke is careful not to distract from the humanity of Christ and the social appeal of the Savior.

The key components of this parable must be properly identified if we are to understand its meaning:

The King of heaven = God.

The Son to be married = Christ.

The wedding feast = the celebration of Christ with His redeemed.

The first invitation = by prophets, John, and Christ Himself.

The second invitation = by disciples to Jews in Jerusalem (Acts 1-8).

City of murderers destroyed = Rome's destruction of Jerusalem in 70 A.D.

The third invitation = general decree to all nations (fulfills Gen. 12:3).

The wedding hall = heaven.

The proper wedding garment = being adorned with Christ's righteousness.

The guest without a wedding garment = a false professor.

The meaning of this parable is fairly transparent. The Jewish nation had repeatedly rejected the offer of God's Son, the Lord Jesus, as their Messiah. After Christ's death and resurrection, God would take His offer of grace in Christ to the Gentiles. After the Church Age began, the message was first proclaimed in Jerusalem and then quickly swept across the Roman Empire. The Holy Spirit wooed a Gentile Bride to Christ, a work that He is still engaged in today. Favored and privileged Israel was judged by God in 70 A.D. The Romans destroyed much of Jerusalem and the temple and the entire Levitical system that Christ replaced was put away. Israel will remain in spiritual blindness until Christ's second coming to the earth. But before the Jewish nation is restored to God, redeemed Gentiles from all over the world will be blessed to feast at God's banqueting table in heaven. This event occurs after the rapture of the Church and the *Judgment Seat of Christ* directly afterwards.

The faithful servants in verse 3 are clearly saved as shown by their good works; however, as the Lord had already taught (Matt. 7:21-23), not everyone professing Christ is truly saved. How is this shown in this parable? The answer is in the wedding garments of the attendees.

A believer who is justified in Christ has God's righteousness imputed to his or her account (2 Cor. 5:21). Figuratively, then, true believers are clothed in God's righteousness. It was customary for the host to provide the guest with a wedding garment if they had none – without Christ this guest was spiritually naked and thus deserving of God's judgment. In Revelation 19:8, the Bride of Christ is wearing white linen garments which reflects the righteousness of Christ. Because the garments in this text refer to the righteous acts of those in Christ for Christ, both the positional and practical righteousness of the believer is portrayed, for true faith has good works to substantiate it (Jas. 2:17). The parable indicates that though all are called by God, only those trusting in Christ for righteousness are chosen to be with God.

The Ten Virgins

And Jesus answered and said to them ... "Then the kingdom of heaven shall be likened to ten virgins who took their lamps and went out to meet the bridegroom. Now five of them were wise, and five were foolish. Those who were foolish took their lamps and took no oil with them, but the wise took oil in their vessels with their lamps. But while the bridegroom was delayed, they all slumbered and slept."

"And at midnight a cry was heard: 'Behold, the bridegroom is coming; go out to meet him!' Then all those virgins arose and trimmed their lamps. And the foolish said to the wise, 'Give us some of your oil, for our lamps are going out.' But the wise answered, saying, 'No, lest there should not be enough for us and you; but go rather to those who sell, and buy for yourselves.' And while they went to buy, the bridegroom came, and those who were ready went in with him to the wedding; and the door was shut."

"Afterward the other virgins came also, saying, 'Lord, Lord, open to us!' But he answered and said, 'Assuredly, I say to you, I do not know you.' Watch therefore, for you know neither the day nor the hour in which the Son of Man is coming" (Matt. 24:4, 25:1-13).

The Tuesday before Calvary was an incredibly busy day for the Lord Jesus. Besides mastering the verbal challenges of the Herodians, the Sadducees, the Pharisees, the scribes, and a lawyer, He also spoke the "Woe" message to the Pharisees and told several parables. After these activities, the Lord departed with His disciples to the Mount of Olives for a time of private ministry.

While the Lord Jesus was speaking to His disciples on the Mount of Olives, they asked Him to reveal to them, *"What will be the sign of Your coming, and of the end of the age?"* (Matt. 24:3). He then proclaimed to them important details concerning the future of Israel and the time of His second coming to the earth. The Lord identified signs associated with the coming of the Tribulation Period, the first half of the Tribulation Period, the Abomination of Desolation in the middle of the Tribulation Period, then the Great Tribulation (speaking of the last half), and of His second advent. The Lord's teachings in this passage are generally chronological and *strictly* Jewish. Because the Church will already be in heaven before the events of the Tribulation Period begin, the events of this passage do not pertain to the Church Age (i.e., except for the escalating signs occurring just prior to the Tribulation Period).

In the Tribulation, the beast (the Antichrist) and the false prophet will be working great signs and wonders to deceive the inhabitants of the world (Rev. 13) – so much so that at the Lord's second advent, the behavior of man will be similar to that in Noah's day. Sexual perversion and unceasing wickedness will characterize humanity's behavior prior to God's judgment, which is not expected.

This is why the Lord did not tell His disciples to be looking for the Antichrist, but rather to be intently watching and waiting for His unannounced return to the air to take the Church home (1 Cor. 1:7-8; 1 Thess. 4:13-18, 5:9; 2 Thess. 1:10). Afterwards, during the Tribulation Period, many Jews will be living for the moment and not expecting Jesus Christ to return as their Messiah. These represent the five virgins without oil and will perish during the Tribulation Period.

The key components of this parable are as follows:

The groom = Christ.

The lamps = a testimony of truth.

The ten virgins = those with Messianic hope in the Tribulation Period.

The oil = the working of the Holy Spirit.

The five virgins with oil = the true remnant at Christ's coming.

The five virgins without oil = superficial faith, do not enter the Kingdom.

The bride = the Church.

The "then" in verse 1 ties this parable with the events revealed by Christ in Matthew chapter 24. The Jewish people are still waiting for Messiah to come. At the end of the Tribulation Period, He and His Bride (all His redeemed in heaven) will return to the earth with Him (Rev. 19:11-16). The Vulgate version of the Bible states that the Bride is with her Groom when He comes in this parable. This suggests that the wedding has already occurred in heaven and that the Bride and the Groom are returning to the earth for the marriage supper, and all that will enter Christ's kingdom will be attending the festivities.

It seems likely, given the Jewish tenor of this passage, that the ten virgins represent the Jewish people scattered among the nations during the Tribulation Period. However, given that the Kingdom gospel is preached throughout the world at this time, the ten virgins may have a wider representation of all those who have Messianic hope, including

Gentiles. Yet, there is nothing in Scripture to suggest that Gentiles refusing to worship the Antichrist receive the Holy Spirit before entering the Kingdom Age. Many Old Testament prophets do, however, foretell that God will pour out His Spirit on the entire Jewish nation at that time (Joel 2:28-29; Ezek. 37:1-14, 39:25-29).

It is noted that all ten virgins slept prior to the Groom's return, which indicates that there was not much difference in their outward behavior while they were waiting for the marriage feast. The critical difference is that five virgins had true Messianic hope in Jesus Christ and had received the Holy Spirit, while others had a mere profession of that truth. No doubt some of these "oil-less" virgins were holding to an erroneous view of the Messiah, which much of Judaism embraces today.

The prophet Zechariah foretold that two-thirds of all Jews will die during this timeframe (Zech. 13:8-9), but those remaining will receive the Holy Spirit and gladly worship Jesus Christ at His second coming (Zech. 12:20). This realization would bolster the idea that the ten virgins (as a minimum) represent the Jewish nation during the Tribulation Period. That is, many Jews will not believe that Jesus Christ is their Messiah and will perish.

As previously mentioned, olive oil is a type of the Holy Spirit in Scripture (Zech. 4:2-6). The light from one's lamp speaks of his or her testimony for God (Matt. 5:14-16). It is only possible to have a true testimony for God when the Holy Spirit is enabling us to live for Christ. The Holy Spirit indwells those who are Christ's; His presence cannot be purchased with money (Eph. 1:13-14).

The five Spirit-filled virgins were watching and waiting for Jesus Christ's return. These true believers were welcomed to celebrate with Christ and His Bride at the wedding feast. At this time Christ will vindicate His name on earth, and punish all those who followed the Antichrist; this is called *The Judgment of Nations* (Rev. 19:17-21). *The Judgment of Nations* is done suddenly and the general populace will not be expecting it (Matt. 24:36-41).

This same judgment is pictured in the analogy of Christ separating the sheep and the goats a little later in this same discourse (Matt. 25:31-46). Those following the Antichrist (the goats) will be executed, while Gentile survivors who were kind to the oppressed Jewish peoples and did not take the beast's mark (the sheep) will enter Christ's Kingdom. The goats suffer death and will wait in Hades for their resurrection and final judgment at *The Great While Throne Judgment* (Rev. 20:11-15). The other five virgins, though waiting for Messiah to come, were not looking for Jesus Christ to return to rule over them. These individuals did not receive the Holy Spirit and therefore were not saved from judgment; they did not enter Christ's Kingdom as the five virgins with oil (i.e., those having the Holy Spirit) did.

It is noted that most of the prophetic books in the Old Testament foretell a future day when the Messiah will come and restore the nation of Israel to Himself. From this viewpoint, Jehovah is the faithful Husband waiting for the restoration of His unfaithful wife, Israel (Jer. 3:8; Hos. 3). In this sense, the ten virgins in this parable seem to equate with the *"daughters of Jerusalem"* referred to in the Song of Solomon (Song. 1:5, 2:2, 2:7, 3:5…). These represent the Jewish nation which is presently spiritually estranged from Jehovah, while the Church is presently the spotless Bride patiently waiting to be united with her Beloved, the Lord Jesus Christ (Eph. 1:6).

The Doorkeeper

> *"But of that day and hour no one knows, not even the angels in heaven, nor the Son, but only the Father. Take heed, watch and pray; for you do not know when the time is. It is like a man going to a far country, who left his house and gave authority to his servants, and to each his work, and commanded the doorkeeper to watch. Watch therefore, for you do not know when the master of the house is coming—in the evening, at midnight, at the crowing of the rooster, or in the morning—lest, coming suddenly, he find you sleeping. And what I say to you, I say to all: Watch!"* (Mark 13:34-37).

This story was spoken privately by the Lord to His disciples as part of the *Olivet Discourse* and likely directly followed the parable of *The Ten Virgins.*

Christ is likened to a man traveling far from home who assigns his servants various tasks and tells them to keep busy until he returns. There is also a doorkeeper who is appointed to watch over and protect the entrance into the house. Though the master had specifically assigned various tasks, the charge to watch for the master's coming was given to all collectively.

All the Lord's servants are to be alert while faithfully laboring for Him. This means that all believers should be anticipating Christ's imminent return. Some servants, such as church elders, are appointed as doorkeepers of Christ's household. These are to oversee and protect those who are otherwise busy doing their assigned tasks.

Although the Lord had just revealed escalating signs of the coming Tribulation Period and His future return to the earth, these were for Israel, not for the Church. There are no specific prophetic signs given to the Church concerning Christ's coming to the air to snatch His Bride to heaven.

The signs that Christ had just mentioned to His disciples would be of great encouragement to the Jewish people suffering under the Antichrist during the Tribulation Period. However, the Church does not know when Christ is returning. His imminent return means that faithful believers should be constantly watching while faithfully serving.

Reward for the Faithful

Parable Title	Reference
The Shrewd Manager	Luke 16:1-9
The Servants' Reward	Luke 17:7-10
The Workers in the Vineyard	Matt. 20:1-16
The Minas (Pounds)	Luke 19:11-27
The Two Servants	Matt. 24:45-51; Luke 12:42-48
The Talents	Matt. 25:14-30

The parables spoken by Christ in the final weeks of His ministry were largely to excite the faithful about the rewards they would receive at His second coming. The next parable of study, *The Shrewd Manager*, accentuates this point by affirming that the Lord expects His disciples to serve Him with eternity in mind; they were not to live for themselves or for the moment.

The Shrewd Manager

He also said to His disciples: "There was a certain rich man who had a steward, and an accusation was brought to him that this man was wasting his goods. So he called him and said to him, 'What is this I hear about you? Give an account of your stewardship, for you can no longer be steward.' Then the steward said within himself, 'What shall I do? For my master is taking the stewardship away from me. I cannot dig; I am ashamed to beg. I have resolved what to do, that when I am put out of the stewardship, they may receive me into their houses.'"

"So he called every one of his master's debtors to him, and said to the first, 'How much do you owe my master?' And he said, 'A hundred measures of oil.' So he said to him, 'Take your bill, and sit down quickly and write fifty.' Then he said to another, 'And how much do you owe?' So he said, 'A hundred measures of wheat.' And he said to him, 'Take your bill, and write eighty.' So the master commended the unjust steward because he had dealt shrewdly. For the sons of this world are more shrewd in their generation than the sons of light."

> *"And I say to you, make friends for yourselves by unrighteous mammon, that when you fail, they may receive you into an everlasting home. He who is faithful in what is least is faithful also in much; and he who is unjust in what is least is unjust also in much. Therefore if you have not been faithful in the unrighteous mammon, who will commit to your trust the true riches? And if you have not been faithful in what is another man's, who will give you what is your own?"*
>
> *"No servant can serve two masters; for either he will hate the one and love the other, or else he will be loyal to the one and despise the other. You cannot serve God and mammon"* (Luke 16:1-13).

This parable was spoken during the Lord's Perean ministry just before the resurrection of His friend Lazarus. The timing would have been during the winter of 30 A.D., two or three months before Calvary.

The story identifies an unfaithful steward who was caught embezzling his master's wealth. The corrupt manager knew that he would soon be required to give an account to his master, and that he could not hide his guilt. He concluded that he was too old to dig ditches for a living and too proud to beg for mercy, so he came up with an innovative plan to ensure his livelihood after being fired by his master.

The shrewd manager quickly went to several clients who owed his master debts and settled their accounts for much less than what was owed. He did not pocket these funds, but rather gained a good standing with those he had just helped – the idea being that these individuals would think favorably of Him and give him assistance after being fired from his job.

It is noteworthy that the rich man in the parable did not commend his evil servant for his theft, but for having enough foresight to look ahead to the future and plan accordingly. He sacrificed present assets for future gain. Believers should also be future thinking and not just living for the moment. Investments into eternity are not really sacrifices because God uses these to honor His name, to further His kingdom on earth, and to reward the faithful with much more than they ever donated back to God previously.

The Lord Jesus told His disciples to use their money wisely to further His cause in the world before their money inevitably lost its value. If they chose not to obey this command, it would indicate that they were mastered by money and not by Him. Eventually, all that is on the earth will be burned up (2 Pet. 3:10; Rev. 21:1-2), so obviously any acquired earthly wealth will be lost. The Lord's point was, "Why invest into that which will be soon destroyed?" It is better to invest one's life into what will endure forever, where neither moth, nor rust, nor thieves can diminish its value (Matt. 5:19-20). Those who choose to invest into eternity have the promise that "*their works follow them*" (Rev. 14:13).

What is the application of this parable for us then? We should use the resources that God supplies us to purchase gospel tracts, Bibles, and evangelistic tools that can be used to win souls for Christ. Additionally, we should support the Lord's servants engaged in evangelical work and strive to supply the practical needs of others in the name of Christ. By laboring to win souls for Christ, we establish friendships that will last for eternity and our heavenly reward for doing so will follow us too!

The Lord then reminded His disciples that the test of faithfulness begins in "what is least" (i.e., in what is often thought of as insignificant responsibilities). The Lord puts value on those seemingly obscure tasks that often have no visible honor. None of us were born with discipline, but we learn discipline by doing what we know we should, even when we do not feel like it. This type of learned discipline accomplishes what good intentions cannot and continues to motivate service when difficulties arise because we want the Lord's approval in all that we do, even in the least of things. May we keep busy, even in mundane tasks of life, wherever the Lord has us in training for reigning. Relish every occasion to please the Lord and to show Him to others in what we do.

The daily matters of life matter as long as we do everything for the Lord and for the honor of His name. The Lord provides greater opportunities for service as His people are faithful to what they have already been asked to do (Luke 16:10-11). There is no example in Scripture where the Lord called a lazy person to serve Him. Elisha was plowing behind twelve yoke of oxen when he received his call from Elijah. Moses and David were shepherding sheep when God beckoned them to service. Gideon was summoned while threshing wheat. Four of the disciples were fishing when they were told by the Lord Jesus, "Follow Me."

The Servants' Reward

So the Lord said ... "And which of you, having a servant plowing or tending sheep, will say to him when he has come in from the field,

'Come at once and sit down to eat'? But will he not rather say to him, 'Prepare something for my supper, and gird yourself and serve me till I have eaten and drunk, and afterward you will eat and drink'? Does he thank that servant because he did the things that were commanded him? I think not. So likewise you, when you have done all those things which you are commanded, say, 'We are unprofitable servants. We have done what was our duty to do'" (Luke 17:6-10).

Returning to the master's home after laboring all day in the field, a servant does not expect his master to cause him to sit down to eat a meal. Rather, the servant puts on an apron and serves his master supper without any praise or thanks from his master. Only after the master is satisfied will the servant be able to eat and rest from the long day.

Servants who have labored long in their assigned tasks do not expect special treatment by their master – they have merely done what was expected of them. In explaining the meaning of the parable, notice that the Lord does not call His servants unprofitable when they have done all that has been requested of them. Rather, it is the disciples who call themselves "unprofitable servants" even when they have done their best to please their Lord.

This is the main point of the parable. Understanding their own unworthiness, true servants of Christ have no reason to be proud or feel self-important. In recognizing all that Christ suffered on our behalf at Calvary to secure our redemption, we consider ourselves a bad investment. Yet, the Lord demonstrated His love for His Father and for us by suffering and dying in our place as guilty sinners – the Lord does consider us valuable to Him.

We realize that our salvation in Christ is an extreme display of divine grace and mercy that can never be repaid by any amount of faithful service (i.e., good works). In utter amazement of Christ's selfless sacrifice, true believers will want to serve the Lord out of the spirit of love, rather than being compelled by a sense of duty. Love and appreciation for Christ prompt joyful service, while merely doing what we are obligated to do often leads to spiritual weariness and regret.

The Two Servants

And Jesus said and answered them ... "Who then is a faithful and wise servant, whom his master made ruler over his household, to give

> *them food in due season? Blessed is that servant whom his master, when he comes, will find so doing. Assuredly, I say to you that he will make him ruler over all his goods. But if that evil servant says in his heart, 'My master is delaying his coming,' and begins to beat his fellow servants, and to eat and drink with the drunkards, the master of that servant will come on a day when he is not looking for him and at an hour that he is not aware of, and will cut him in two and appoint him his portion with the hypocrites. There shall be weeping and gnashing of teeth"* (Matt. 24:4, 45-51).

Luke also records this parable which was spoken privately to the disciples on the Mount of Olives the Tuesday before Christ's crucifixion (Luke 12:42-48). The disciples did not understand that there would be a long period of time between the Lord's advents to the earth. Several of the Lord's final parables emphasized that His disciples should not lose heart during this interim which would be marked by hardship.

This story was told to exhort the disciples to be faithful to Him after His departure. They and the following generations of disciples that would believe their message were to show love to Christ by properly caring for His people. Loyal and wise servants would be amply rewarded when He returned to examine their faithfulness to what they had been entrusted. The Lord's sheep (His people) are not always easy to love and to serve with joy, but they are His Beloved, thus we should care for them regardless of how much they glare, smell, kick, bite, and wander.

A few moments later the Lord Jesus would be teaching His disciples about *The Judgment of Nations* (the sorting of the sheep and the goats) at the end of the Tribulation Period. The Sheep, the righteous permitted to enter Christ's kingdom in the analogy, did not understand the King's accolade about them caring for Him, so He clarified the matter: *"And the King will answer and say to them, 'Assuredly, I say to you, inasmuch as you did it to one of the least of these My brethren, you did it to Me'"* (Matt. 25:40). In application, the way we treat the lowliest believer in the Body of Christ shows our true esteem for the Lord Jesus Christ.

Our tendency is to rub shoulders with those of status and that are well-to-do and snub those of humble estate. We tend to avoid identifying and associating with those who are burdened, persecuted, and suffering. But all believers are one in Christ; we all are members of His Body, of His Church, and compose His Bride. When one member of the Body suffers – all of its members suffer. This spiritual reality must compel us to have the same care for one another that Christ would have for us (1 Cor. 12:25-26).

The Workers in the Vineyard

> *So Jesus said to them ... "For the kingdom of heaven is like a landowner who went out early in the morning to hire laborers for his vineyard. Now when he had agreed with the laborers for a denarius a day, he sent them into his vineyard. And he went out about the third hour and saw others standing idle in the marketplace, and said to them, 'You also go into the vineyard, and whatever is right I will give you.' So they went. Again he went out about the sixth and the ninth hour, and did likewise. And about the eleventh hour he went out and found others standing idle, and said to them, 'Why have you been standing here idle all day?' They said to him, 'Because no one hired us.' He said to them, 'You also go into the vineyard, and whatever is right you will receive.'"*
>
> *"So when evening had come, the owner of the vineyard said to his steward, 'Call the laborers and give them their wages, beginning with the last to the first.' And when those came who were hired about the eleventh hour, they each received a denarius. But when the first came, they supposed that they would receive more; and they likewise received each a denarius. And when they had received it, they complained against the landowner, saying, 'These last men have worked only one hour, and you made them equal to us who have borne the burden and the heat of the day.' But he answered one of them and said, 'Friend, I am doing you no wrong. Did you not agree with me for a denarius? Take what is yours and go your way. I wish to give to this last man the same as to you. Is it not lawful for me to do what I wish with my own things? Or is your eye evil because I am good?' So the last will be first, and the first last. For many are called, but few chosen"* (Matt. 19:28, 20:1-16).

Peter had just asked the Lord Jesus a bold question concerning rewards for being loyal to Him: *"We have given up everything for you. What shall we have?"* (Matt. 19:28-29). Surprisingly, the Lord did not rebuke Peter, but merely cautioned him about his motives. The Lord then affirmed that they would be highly honored and given authority in His kingdom. Additionally, they would possess eternal life and even now could expect a hundredfold increase for every relationship severed by the gospel.

It is the same for believers today. For every person who persecutes a believer, there will be a hundred more believers to lend him or her a helping hand. Christian love is a powerful weapon against the enemy, for it conveys the reality of the gospel message to the lost. May we all give thanks to the Lord for all the gracious benefits of a loving community of saints during our earthly sojourn. Indeed, rewards will be received at the *Judgment Seat of Christ*, but we can assist each other to be faithful to Christ until that day.

This parable was told in the Spring of 30 A.D. during the Perean ministry. The Lord and His disciples were nearing the Jordan River on their way to Jericho. This story was told as an additional response to Peter's question, "What shall we have?"

A landowner, looking for laborers to work in his vineyard, negotiated with several laborers at 6:00 A.M. to work a full day in his vineyard for a denarius. Afterwards, the landowner found men standing in the marketplace at 9 A.M, Noon, 3 P.M., and 5 P.M. These men wanted to work, but no one would hire them, so the landowner compelled them to go and work in his vineyard and he would pay them "what was right." These workers eagerly went to the vineyard and labored for various lengths of time without knowing what they would receive at the end of the day as a wage.

At the end of the workday, the foreman paid the laborers in the reverse order that they had been summoned. Surprisingly, everyone received the same wage – a denarius. Those who had worked an entire day in the vineyard supposed that they would have received more from the landowner, since the latecomers were paid a full day's wage. These workers therefore complained against the landowner, but he reminded them that they had received what they had agreed to earn for their laboring.

There are at least three important applications from this parable that we should consider. First, we understand that believers are given different opportunities to serve the Lord. Some receive Christ later in life, while others are hampered by mental and physical limitations. It is comforting to know that at the *Judgment Seat of Christ*, the Lord will reward saints for faithfulness to the opportunities into which they have been entrusted. A middle-aged convert who lives vibrantly for Christ the remainder of his or her life will not receive a diminished reward. It is our faithfulness to the opportunities Christ gives to further His kingdom that is important, not how long we have been a Christian or even how faithful we were to the more glamorous opportunities afforded to us. We cannot pick and choose what we want to do for Christ. Rather, He rewards us for faithfulness to do what He puts before us and in the season that He provides for us to accomplish it.

Second, the Lord Jesus will reward us far beyond what we deserve for being faithful to the opportunities that He does give us to serve Him. We need not compare our ministries to those of others, for servants are not to judge each other in this manner – only the Master will judge the value of our service (Rom. 14:4). Each of us must give an account to Christ for what we do, not what others do.

Third, we should not presuppose to what extent that the Lord will reward each of us for faithful service. What rewards that He does bestow at the *Judgment Seat of Christ* will be a reflective glory of Himself that will give us a greater appreciation of heaven and opportunity to worship Christ forever. While all believers in the Church have been positionally declared righteous in Christ, each believer has the opportunity to labor in righteousness for Christ. Those things which are done in accordance with revealed truth and in the power of the Holy Spirit have eternal value. As previously mentioned, the outshining of these righteous acts is what the believer is adorned with throughout eternity (Rev. 19:7-8).

After glorification, some saints will shine brighter than others, just as some stars in the nighttime sky are more brilliant than others (1 Cor. 15:40-42). This acquired glory directly reflects the righteous acts (good works) that are done for Christ presently (Rev. 19:8). Eternal glory has a weight to it; in other words, its quality is measurable (2 Cor. 4:17) and can be earned by believers through selfless service for Christ now. May we be faithful to all the opportunities Christ affords us to serve Him now!

The Ten Minas (Pounds)

> *Now as they heard these things, He spoke another parable, because He was near Jerusalem and because they thought the kingdom of God would appear immediately. Therefore He said: "A certain nobleman*

went into a far country to receive for himself a kingdom and to return. So he called ten of his servants, delivered to them ten minas, and said to them, 'Do business till I come.' But his citizens hated him, and sent a delegation after him, saying, 'We will not have this man to reign over us.'"

"And so it was that when he returned, having received the kingdom, he then commanded these servants, to whom he had given the money, to be called to him, that he might know how much every man had gained by trading. Then came the first, saying, 'Master, your mina has earned ten minas.' And he said to him, 'Well done, good servant; because you were faithful in a very little, have authority over ten cities.' And the second came, saying, 'Master, your mina has earned five minas.' Likewise he said to him, 'You also be over five cities.'"

"Then another came, saying, 'Master, here is your mina, which I have kept put away in a handkerchief. For I feared you, because you are an austere man. You collect what you did not deposit, and reap what you did not sow.' And he said to him, 'Out of your own mouth I will judge you, you wicked servant. You knew that I was an austere man, collecting what I did not deposit and reaping what I did not sow. Why then did you not put my money in the bank, that at my coming I might have collected it with interest?'"

"And he said to those who stood by, 'Take the mina from him, and give it to him who has ten minas.' (But they said to him, 'Master, he has ten minas.') 'For I say to you, that to everyone who has will be given; and from him who does not have, even what he has will be taken away from him. But bring here those enemies of mine, who did not want me to reign over them, and slay them before me'" (Luke 19:11-27).

As the Lord and His disciples had entered into and passed through Jericho (Luke 19:1) and were nearing Jerusalem (Luke 19:11), this parable would have been told shortly after *The Workers in the Vineyard* parable. The Lord's life-changing conversation with Zacchaeus near Jericho occurred between these two parables.

In the parable of *The Ten Minas*, the master gave each of his ten servants one mina (worth about 100 denarii) to invest while he was on a long journey. The disciples believed that Christ's earthly kingdom would be soon, but this parable was to teach them that there would be a long interim between His first and second advents. During this time believers in the Church Age would have the opportunity to invest into Christ's kingdom. When He does return, each servant will give an account of their stewardship to Him. This will occur at the *Judgment Seat of Christ* directly after the rapture of the Church, but before the Tribulation Period and Christ's second coming to the earth.

In the story, all servants were given the same amount to invest during the interim that the master was away. Yet, the servants had varying success depending on their degree of faithfulness. In the Church Age, all believers receive differing spiritual gifts and abilities, and prospects to serve, but this parable deals with those things we are all given equal *availability* to. For example, all believers are given the gospel message to share, the same amount of time each day to work, mutual access to God through prayer, and the same access to God's Word. However, not all believers will use what God has made available to them for serving Him in the same way. As an example, many Christians have homes, but few use what God has given them to show hospitality to others, though we are expected to do so (1 Pet. 4:9-10).

One servant earned ten pounds and was rewarded with ten cities to rule, while a second servant made five pounds and was given five cities. The slothful servant, who did not appreciate the true character of his master, lost the mina given him and received no reward. A person may be a Christian, but choose to waste his or her life – living a life without any concern for what God wants. Such unfaithful believers will lose what they were given, which will be given to the faithful person with proven devotion. This is how a Christian may lose the crown they could have received at the *Judgment Seat of Christ* (Rev. 3:11). Let us be found faithful to what the Lord has graciously entrusted us with. If we are unsure how to invest what the Lord has given us, may we entrust it to those who do, so both we and those investing can be rewarded for the profitable outcome.

As this parable relates to the Church Age, the dispensation of grace between Christ's two earthly advents, it is suggested that the individuals who did not want Christ to rule over them represent the religious Jews at that time. In 70 A.D. the obsolete religious system under the Law was abruptly put away by the destruction of much of Jerusalem and the temple by the Romans. Judaism today continues to be an affront to God's message of salvation in Jesus Christ; thus, the

Jewish people will continue to suffer in spiritual blindness until a remnant is refined and revived during the Tribulation Period.

The Lord has given each believer different abilities and opportunities to serve, but we have all been given equal availability to a variety of things: twenty-four hours each day to use, the Word of God to study, the gospel message to share, access to the throne of grace to pray, and food, clothing, and homes to share. Some will take greater advantage of the Throne of Grace than others will and some will use their time more frugally than others will and thus receive a greater reward. How available are you to serve?

The Talents

> *And Jesus answered and said to them ... "For the kingdom of heaven is like a man traveling to a far country, who called his own servants and delivered his goods to them. And to one he gave five talents, to another two, and to another one, to each according to his own ability; and immediately he went on a journey. Then he who had received the five talents went and traded with them, and made another five talents. And likewise he who had received two gained two more also. But he who had received one went and dug in the ground, and hid his lord's money. After a long time the lord of those servants came and settled accounts with them."*
>
> *"So he who had received five talents came and brought five other talents, saying, 'Lord, you delivered to me five talents; look, I have gained five more talents besides them.' His lord said to him, 'Well done, good and faithful servant; you were faithful over a few things, I will make you ruler over many things. Enter into the joy of your lord.' He also who had received two talents came and said, 'Lord, you delivered to me two talents; look, I have gained two more talents besides them.' His lord said to him, 'Well done, good and faithful servant; you have been faithful over a few things, I will make you ruler over many things. Enter into the joy of your lord.'"*
>
> *"Then he who had received the one talent came and said, 'Lord, I knew you to be a hard man, reaping where you have not sown, and gathering where you have not scattered seed. And I was afraid, and went and hid your talent in the ground. Look, there you have what is yours.'"*

> *"But his lord answered and said to him, 'You wicked and lazy servant, you knew that I reap where I have not sown, and gather where I have not scattered seed. So you ought to have deposited my money with the bankers, and at my coming I would have received back my own with interest. So take the talent from him, and give it to him who has ten talents. For to everyone who has, more will be given, and he will have abundance; but from him who does not have, even what he has will be taken away. And cast the unprofitable servant into the outer darkness. There will be weeping and gnashing of teeth'"* (Matt. 24:4, 25:14-30).

The Lord was with His disciples on the Mount of Olives the Tuesday evening before Calvary when He spoke this parable. He was teaching them about the Tribulation Period and His second coming, in response to their question to know more about future events.

In the story of *The Talents*, a man was preparing for an extended journey into a far country. He set his household in order and committed his substance into the hands of his servants. In his wisdom he gave one servant five talents, another two, and another one, *"to each according to his particular ability"* (Matt. 25:15, Darby). There would be much accountability for each servant's stewardship, as a talent was 58 to 80 pounds of silver worth 6000 denarii. A talent represented about twenty years of wages for a common laborer.

After the master departed, the servant with five talents earned double that amount through wise investments. The servant who had been given two talents also doubled his talents in the same way. However, the servant who had received one talent buried it in the earth. He decided to reserve and return what his master had given to him, but without any benefit of having received it.

When the householder returned, the first two servants reported the increase and delivered the ten and four talents, respectively. The master heartily praised each of them with the same words: *"Well done, good and faithful servant; you were faithful over a few things, I will make you ruler over many things. Enter into the joy of your lord"* (Matt. 25:21, 23). Then the last servant came before the householder. After calling his master harsh and unfair, he returned the single talent that he had received without any earnings.

The master then addressed him as a *"wicked and lazy servant,"* and rebuked his slothfulness. If he personally did not want to use the talent to earn a profit, he should have deposited it in a bank, so at least the talent would have earned some interest. In the end, the last servant's lone talent is entrusted to the one who had ten, and the servant himself is thrown out into the outer darkness where there is weeping and gnashing of teeth (this speaks of eternal judgment in Hell).

The *Olivet Discourse* of Matthew chapters 24-25 is Jewish in focus and is speaking of the Tribulation Period and Christ's second coming. During the Tribulation Period the Kingdom gospel message will be preached throughout the world (Matt. 24:14). The Jewish people will be refined and restored to God towards the conclusion of this horrific time.

The Kingdom message is what Christ preached to Israel initially, but was rejected; it was the offer of a literal, earthly, political kingdom (Matt. 4:17). Today, the Church preaches the gospel of grace: Christ crucified and raised from death for our justification. Only believers are tasked by the Lord with sharing this message with the lost (Matt. 28:19-20). There is no example in Scripture of even angels intruding on this responsibility. After the Church Age has concluded, the Kingdom message will be preached again in Israel and indeed throughout the world. John foretold that angels would then fly over the earth to publicly declare its validity – the true King is coming to judge; do not worship the Antichrist (Rev. 14:6-12).

The time setting in which this parable is associated is crucial to understanding its meaning. Every person has been given abilities by God to be used for His honor and glory. Those who reject His offer of salvation will not use their natural abilities to serve God and thus live a wasted life. In this parable the third servant represents this type of person. Someone who is ignorant of God's character, attributes, word, etc. will not live for Him. God does not force Himself on anyone, but permits us to choose life in Him or death apart from Him.

This coldhearted servant did not want to do anything to benefit his master. Unfaithful servants are so because they do not trust their Lord's character and they do not realize the Lord's claim on them. This is why the unfaithful servant grudgingly returned the single talent and said, *"There you have what is yours."* The servant was smugly declaring to his master, "You own the talent, but you do not own me!"

During the Tribulation Period, those living on the planet will have to choose God and His Lamb or the Antichrist; those aligning with the Antichrist will ultimately be cast into Hell (speaking of the *Lake of*

Fire). This understanding explains why the unprofitable servant in this parable, an unbeliever, was cast into eternal judgment, but the unprofitable servant in the parable of *The Minas* (a despondent believer in the Church Age) only lost his reward. The parables relate to two different economies of truth in which man has been entrusted to respond by faith (this is called a "dispensation" in Scripture; Eph. 1:10, 3:2).

The parable shows us that God bestows different "talents" (natural abilities) to each person as He chooses, but everyone has an opportunity to please God with what they have received. Likewise, in the Church Age, Christ has given different individuals to the Church for its edification (Eph. 4:11-12) and that the Holy Spirit bestows spiritual gifts to each believer as He wills (1 Cor. 12:4-11). The tendency of our flesh is to compare our abilities and ministries to each other, but as we learn from this story, eternal reward is given in accordance with faithfulness to use what we have been given, rather than what was actually accomplished.

Paul posed three questions to exhort the carnal Corinthian believers to cease comparing God's servants and their ministries to each other: *"For who makes you differ from another? And what do you have that you did not receive? Now if you did indeed receive it, why do you boast as if you had not received it?"* (1 Cor. 4:7). The answers to these questions respectively are: "God," "Nothing," and "It is foolish to compare or boast about what we have received in God's sovereignty." Hence, believers should be faithful to use what God entrusts to each individual and should not question, compare, or boast about what has been received from God or what others have received from Him. What God alone gives, He alone enables through faith and that is all that matters!

In summary, we are not to compare what we have received by divine grace and wisdom to what others have received. No one should compare the ministries of a one-talent preacher to a five-talent preacher; all that is important is that both preachers faithfully use their God-given abilities for Him. All of our talents received (resources, natural abilities, and spiritual gifts) should be fully devoted to the work of the Lord. When God gives more, He expects more. Accordingly, we see that the first two servants in the parable received exactly the same praise from their master, despite having differing abilities to serve him.

We can expect the Lord Jesus to behave in this gracious manner at the *Judgment Seat of Christ*.

Faithful Servants Will Be Rewarded

Believers will be rewarded for their faithfulness at the *Judgment Seat of Christ*. It is then that the value of our actions will be made clear. With what motive and in whose strength did we serve the Lord? How did we avail ourselves of the throne of grace and God's Word? How did we use our natural abilities, spiritual gifts, time, finances, and possessions to serve the Lord? Were we faithful to share the gospel message with the lost? May we be found faithful when we stand before the Lord Jesus Christ and give an account of ourselves (Rom. 14:10-12; 2 Cor. 5:10).

It is fitting for the Lord to close His parable ministry by speaking of His glorious return to the earth and His eagerness to reward faithful servants. Let us give the Lord our opportunities, abilities and availability, knowing full well that our rewards will directly reflect His glory for eternity and thus enable us to appreciate Him and heaven to a greater extent!

> I know of nothing which I would choose to have as the subject of my ambition for life than to be kept faithful to my God till death.
>
> – C. H. Spurgeon

> God is God. Because He is God, He is worthy of my trust and obedience. I will find rest nowhere but in His holy will, a will that is unspeakably beyond my largest notions of what He is up to.
>
> – Elisabeth Elliot

> The greatest legacy one can pass on to one's children and grandchildren is not money or other material things

accumulated in one's life, but rather a legacy of character and faith.

– Billy Graham

True faith rests upon the character of God and asks no further proof than the moral perfections of the One who cannot lie.

– A.W. Tozer

Summary of Christ's Parables

The Kingdom of Heaven

Parable Title	Reference	Summary
The Sower and the Soils	Matt. 13:5-8; Mark 4:3-8; Luke 8:5-8	The Word has various visible influences on human hearts, but ongoing fruitfulness indicates true faith.
The Wheat and the Tares	Matt. 13:24-30	Satan will try to neutralize a believer's influence.
The Mustard Seed	Matt. 13:31-32; Mark 4:30-32; Luke 13:18-19	The kingdom will have abnormal growth from a simple message, but develop into something which welcomes corrupt leadership and order in the last days.
The Leaven and the Woman	Matt. 13:33; Luke 13:20-21	What is false is put into the food of God's people.
The Hidden Treasure	Matt. 13:44	Israel remains hidden, but will be restored to God.
The Pearl of Great Price	Matt. 13:45-46	The Church is one body – paid for with Christ's blood.
The Dragnet	Matt. 13:47-50	Gentiles not following the Antichrist will enter Christ's kingdom, but everyone else will perish.
Mysterious Growth	Mark 4:26-29	It is God who gives spiritual growth and fruitfulness.

Summary of Christ's Parables

Salvation and Evidence of Salvation

Parable Title	Reference	Summary
The New Cloth/New Wineskin	Matt. 9:16-17	Live by the law or the gospel of grace, but do not mix.
The Two Houses	Matt. 7:24-27; Luke 6:47-49	A true disciple obeys and lives by God's Word.
The Two Debtors	Luke 7:41-43	The forgiven love much; the self-righteous love not.
The Unforgiving Servant	Matt. 18:23-25	God's forgiveness is limitless; let us be forgiving.
The Good Samaritan	Luke 10:25-37	If a Jew in dire need received help from a Samaritan – why not let Christ resolve your need because of sin?
Friend at Midnight/Fatherhood	Luke 11:5-8	God desires more than men do to provide for our needs.
The Rich Fool	Luke 12:16-21	Selfish independent living brings separation from God.
The Great Supper	Luke 14:15-24	All are invited by Christ, but many will make excuses.
The Unfinished Tower/The King's Rash War/Salt	Luke 14:28-33	The cost of being a disciple is everything; Christ wants dedicated/committed learners, not just followers.
The Lost Sheep	Matt. 18:12-14; Luke 15:4-7	Sinners lost by foolishness must repent to be saved.
The Lost Coin	Luke 15:8-10	Sinners lost by carelessness must repent to be saved.
The Lost Son	Luke 15:11-32	Sinners lost by pious legalism must repent to be saved.

Summary of Christ's Parables

The Lord's Second Coming and Jewish Attitudes

Parable Title	Reference	Summary
The Rude Children	Luke 7:31-35	The self-righteous long to find fault with the righteous.
The Barren Fig Tree	Luke 13:6-9	Christ preached to the Jews 3 years without acceptance.
The Unjust Judge	Luke 18:1-8	Pray persistently – God is the One most able to help.
The Pharisee and the Tax Collector	Luke 18:9-14	Repentant with humility, no self-honoring before God.
The Two Sons	Matt. 21:28-32	Rebellious Gentiles will accept Christ; Jews will not.
The Wicked Vinedressers	Matt 21:33-46; Mark 12:1-12; Luke 20:9-19	Proud Israel rebelled against God, His prophets and His Son; they would crucify His Son to keep their approval.
The Marriage of the King's Son	Matt. 22:1-14	Jews would reject Christ, but Gentiles to trust in Him.
The Ten Virgins	Matt. 25:1-13	Only those Jews having the Holy Spirit enter kingdom.
The Doorkeeper	Mark 13:34-37	The time of Christ's coming is unknown; be watchful!

Summary of Christ's Parables

Reward for the Faithful

Parable Title	Reference	Summary
The Shrewd Manager	Luke 16:1-9	Think eternally – do not live for the moment.
The Servants' Reward	Luke 17:7-10	We will never be able to repay Christ for Calvary.
The Workers in the Vineyard	Matt. 20:1-16	Be faithful to what *opportunities* you are given.
The Minas (Pounds)	Luke 19:1-27	Be faithful to *availability* – prayer, gospel, and time.
The Two Servants	Matt. 24:45-51; Luke 12:42-48	Be faithful servants in caring for God's people.
The Talents	Matt. 25:14-30	Be faithful to what *abilities* you are given.

Possible Order of Parables (Assumes Calvary Was in 30 A.D.)

Parable	Location	When	Comment
The New Cloth & New Wineskin	Capernaum	Spring 28 AD	Just before 2nd Passover & Sermon on the Mount; answered John's disciples' query about fasting.
Note: The Lord had between one and one and a half years of ministry before telling a parable.			
The Two Houses	Near Capernaum	Spring 28 AD	Spoken to crowd; ends the Sermon on the Mount.
The Rude Children	Galilee	Spring 28 AD	Spoken to crowd; confronted the self-righteous.
The Two Debtors	Capernaum	Mid 28 AD	In response to Simon's (a Pharisee) thoughts.
The Sower	Sea of Galilee	Late 28 AD	Revealed kingdom mysteries to a large crowd.
The Seed Growing Secretly	Sea of Galilee	Late 28 AD	Revealed kingdom mysteries to a large crowd.
The Tares	Sea of Galilee	Late 28 AD	Revealed kingdom mysteries to a large crowd.
The Mustard Seed	Sea of Galilee	Late 28 AD	Revealed kingdom mysteries to a large crowd.
The Yeast	Sea of Galilee	Late 28 AD	Revealed kingdom mysteries to a large crowd.
The Hidden Treasure	Sea of Galilee	Late 28 AD	Revealed kingdom mysteries to a large crowd.
The Pearl of Great Price	Sea of Galilee	Late 28 AD	Revealed kingdom mysteries to a large crowd.
The Fishing Net	Sea of Galilee	Late 28 AD	Revealed kingdom mysteries to a large crowd.
Note: The above eight parables were spoken on one day.			

Possible Order of Parables (Assumes Calvary Was in 30 A.D.)

Parable	Location	When	Comment
The Unforgiving Servant	Capernaum	Late 29 AD	Responded to Peter's question on forgiving.
Note: Ends two-year Galilean Ministry; in almost 2 and 1/2 years of ministry the Lord spoke 13 Parables.			
The Good Samaritan	Judea	Fall 29 AD	Response to lawyer: "Who is my neighbor?"
Friend at Midnight/ Fatherhood	Judea	Fall 29 AD	Response to a disciple's plea "teach us to pray."
The Rich Fool	Judea	Fall 29 AD	Spoken to crowd before the Feast of Dedication.
The Barren Fig Tree	Judea	Fall 29 AD	Focusing on Jews; just before Perean Ministry.
The Great Supper	Perea	Winter 29-30 AD	Spoken in a Pharisee's home – lawyers present.
The Unfinished Tower & King's Rash War & Salt	Perea	Winter 29-30 AD	Spoken to a crowd after the Great Supper story.
The Lost Sheep	Perea	Winter 29-30 AD	Sinners draw near; the religious groan from afar.
The Lost Coin	Perea	Winter 29-30 AD	Sinners draw near; the religious groan from afar.
The Lost Son	Perea	Winter 29-30 AD	Sinners draw near; the religious groan from afar.
The Shrewd Manager	Perea	Winter 30 AD	Spoken to disciples before Lazarus' resurrection.
The Servants' Reward	Perea	Winter 30 AD	Spoken to disciples before Lazarus' resurrection.
The Unjust Judge	Galilee/Samaria?	Spring 30 AD	Spoken to disciples; ready to go to Jerusalem.

Possible Order of Parables (Assumes Calvary Was in 30 A.D.)

Parable	Location	When	Comment
The Pharisee/Tax Collector	Galilee/Samaria?	Spring 30 AD	Spoken to self-righteous.
The Workers in the Vineyard	Perea	Spring 30 AD	In response to disciples' "What shall we have?" Nearing Jordan River and then on to Jericho.
The Pounds	Leaving Jericho	Spring 30 AD	On His way to Jerusalem and to Calvary.
Note: Christ teaching on rewards mainly occurred in the last couple weeks of His earthy ministry.			
The Two Sons	Jerusalem	Spring 30 AD	Super Tuesday – spoken to the religious leaders.
The Wicked Vinedressers	Jerusalem	Spring 30 AD	Super Tuesday – spoken to the religious leaders.
The Marriage Feast	Jerusalem	Spring 30 AD	Super Tuesday – spoken to the religious leaders.
The Two Servants	Mt. Olives	Spring 30 AD	Spoken to disciples, shortly after above parables.
The Ten Virgins	Mt. Olives	Spring 30 AD	Spoken to disciples, shortly after above parables.
The Talents	Mt. Olives	Spring 30 AD	Spoken to disciples, shortly after above parables.
Doorkeeper	Mt. Olives	Spring 30 AD	Spoken to disciples; concluded Olivet Discourse.

Note: The Lord spoke seven or eight parables in the week prior to Calvary.
Note: The Lord spoke twenty-two parables in the last six months of His earthly ministry.
Note: Often parables were spoken collectively; Scripture indicates all parables spoken on fifteen occasions.

Endnotes

1 Arthur Pink, *Why Four Gospels?* (Scripture Truth Book Co., Fincastle, VA; no date), pp. 162-163

2 J. H. Thayer, *Thayer's Greek Lexicon* (Biblesoft; 2000), electronic database

3 James Strong, *New Exhaustive Strong's Numbers and Concordance With Expanded Greek-Hebrew Dictionary* (Biblesoft and International Bible Translators, Inc.; 1994)

4 C. I. Scofield, *The New Scofield Study Bible* (Oxford University Press, New York; 1967), p. 994; Note 3

5 William MacDonald, *Here's the Difference* (Gospel Folio Press, Port Colborne, ON; 1999), pp. 119-120

6 L. Laurenson, *Classic Christian Commentary* (Books for Christians, Charlotte, NC; no date) p. 44

7 Warren Wiersbe, *The Bible Exposition Commentary* Vol. 1 (Victor Books, Wheaton, IL; 1989), p. 46

8 William MacDonald, *Believer's Bible Commentary* (Thomas Nelson Publishers, Nashville, TN: 1989); p. 1274

9 Ibid.; p. 1394

10 Hillel Geva, *"Jerusalem's Population in Antiquity: A Minimalist View"* (Tel Aviv, 42:2; 2013), pp. 131-160

11 John Wilkinson, "*Ancient Jerusalem, Its Water Supply and Population"* (PEFQS 106; 1974), pp. 33–51

12 Magen Broshi, *"Estimating the Population of Ancient Jerusalem"* (BAR 4:02; June 1978)

OLD TESTAMENT
Devotional Commentary Series

- **Christ-Centered Exposition**
- **Life-Changing Application**
- **Fourteen Volumes**
- **Over 5,400 Pages**
- **Nearly 200 Contributors**

The primary purpose for studying God's Word is to know the Lord and learn how to please Him. The aim of a devotional commentary is to help the reader pause and consider the deeper, life-related implications of the portion being read. What is God telling us about His character, emotions and attributes? How is His plan of salvation being displayed? How should we respond to His Word? Today, the Christian community sits atop a vast array of written resources, many of which have been penned by those who have gone to be with Christ. Though some of these books are out of print, they still display a relevance to current issues while maintaining a deeply devotional viewpoint, sadly lacking in much of today's Christian literature. This *OT Devotional Commentary Series* captures some of the richest gleanings of nearly two hundred time-honored authors whose goal was sound biblical exposition that would magnify Christ and lead to godly living. Each volume contains dozens of brief devotions. This permits the reader to use the series as a daily devotional or as a reference source for deeper study.

— *Warren Henderson*

A New Testament Journey

May We Serve Christ!

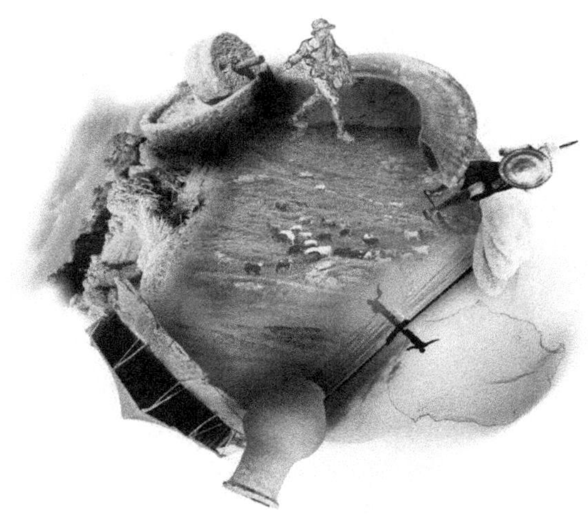

WARREN HENDERSON

At this moment, each of us is as close to the Lord Jesus Christ as we desire to be. Our patient Savior is always ready to assist anyone genuinely seeking Him and desiring to serve Him in his or her appointed capacity and calling. Through His Word and His Spirit, God aids a true seeker every step of the way into a deeper knowledge of Himself and His purposes. *May We Serve Christ? – A New Testament Journey* draws practical application from Scripture to convict, to confront, and to encourage us to *"press toward the goal for the prize of the upward call of God in Christ Jesus"* (Phil. 3:14.). There is a Savior to know, a work to do, a calling to be fulfilled, a race to run, and a higher experience with God to be enjoyed! — Warren Henderson

May We See Christ – An Old Testament Journey is a sequential study of Scripture containing 366 two-page devotions (758 pages). Besides the plain language of the Old Testament, God has employed a variety of types, symbols, and allegories in a complementary fashion to teach us about His Son. With the light of New Testament truth and the illuminating assistance of the Holy Spirit, we are able to understand and appreciate these fascinating Old Testament pictures. All of God's written Word speaks of Christ to some degree as He is the main emphasis of Scripture. Accordingly, the best reason to embark on this one-year journey is to more clearly see, know, and love Christ. May the Lord richly bless your daily contemplations of the Savior as you expectantly peer into God's oracles and witness the glory of His Son. — Warren Henderson